Student Support Materials for
AQA A2 Sociology

Unit 4

Crime and Deviance
with Theory and
Methods

d Liz Steel
er Langley

Published by Collins Education
An imprint of HarperCollins Publishers
77-85 Fulham Palace Road
Hammersmith
London
W6 8JB

Browse the complete Collins Education catalogue at
www.collinseducation.com

10 9 8 7 6 5 4 3 2

ISBN 978-0-00-741834-3

Steve Chapman and Liz Steel assert their moral rights to be identified as the authors of this work.

British Library Cataloguing in Publication Data.

A catalogue record for this publication is available from the British Library.

Commissioned by Charlie Evans and Andrew Campbell

Project editors: Sarah Vittachi and Gudrun Kaiser

Design and typesetting by Hedgehog Publishing Limited

Cover Design by Angela English

Production by Simon Moore

Printed and bound in China

Indexed by Indexing Specialists (UK) Ltd and Gudrun Kaiser

Acknowledgements

Every effort has been made to contact the holders of copyright material, but if any have been inadvertently overlooked the publishers will be pleased to make the necessary arrangements at the first opportunity.

p4, table 1, source: Home Office Crime Statistics; p5, table 2, source: British Crime Survey 2009, ONS; table 3, source: British Crime Survey 2009; study, source: British Crime Survey 2009, ONS; p6, fig 1, source: British Crime Survey 2008, ONS; study, source: Home Office Crime Statistics; p7, table 4, source: British Crime Survey 2008, ONS; fig 2, source: British Crime Survey 2008, ONS; p9, study, source: Home Office Research and Statistics Department (1995), Information on the criminal justice system in England and Wales, HMSO, London, 25; p19, table 6, source: Health and Safety Executive, 1995; p33, study, source: Dick Hobbs *et al.* (2000), Violence in the night-time economy; Bouncers: the reporting, recording and prosecution of assaults, *Policing and Society* (2000), 10 (4): 383–402; p29, study, source: Michele J. Burman, Susan A. Batchelor and Jane A. Brown, Researching Girls and Violence: Facing the Dilemmas of Fieldwork, *British Journal of Criminology* (2001) 41 (3): 443–459, Oxford University Press; p32, study, source: Home Office Crime Statistics; p33, study, source: Offending, Crime and Justice Survey 2003, Home Office; p38–39, study, source: Rob White, 'Green Criminology and the Pursuit of Social and Ecological Justice', eds. P. Bierne & N. South, *Issues in Green Criminology* (2007), Devon: Willan Publishing; p39, study, source: Keith Soothill and Sylvia Walby, *Sex Crime in the News* (2001), Routledge; p44, source: Jason Ditton and James Duffy, 'Bias in the Newspaper Reporting of Crime News', *British Journal of Criminology* (1983), 23 (2), 159–165, Oxford University Press; p53, study, source: HM Prison Service; pp94 and 104, study, source: Home Office Crime Statistics.

Thanks to the following students for providing answers to the questions:

Ruby Barwood, Collette Blackman, Lauren Foley, Vicki Gill, Jessica Gowers, Fran Guratsky, Rachel Hewitt, Ella Keating, Charlotte Ross, Eric Wedge-Bull.

Contents

Patterns of crime and deviance

British sociologists get much of their information about patterns and trends in crime from the official crime statistics (OCS). Published quarterly by the government, these are based on:

- crimes reported by victims and the general public, and recorded by the police
- crimes detected and 'cleared up', or solved, by the police
- crimes reported to the **British Crime Survey (BCS)**. The BCS, introduced in 1983, is an annual **survey** of crime victimization, in which about 47 000 adults aged 16 or over and living in private households in England and Wales are interviewed face-to-face about their experiences as victims of property crimes such as burglary, and personal crimes such as assault.

The BCS is thought to provide a more realistic picture of household and personal crime than the OCS because it includes crimes that are not reported to the police or recorded by them.

The OCS are used to establish trends and patterns in criminal activity, especially to do with:

- the volume of crime – how much of it there is and if it is increasing or decreasing
- the main types of crime – whether or not it takes the form of violence against the person or is property-orientated
- the 'typical' social characteristics of the people who are reported, arrested and convicted of the crime.

The OCS are also useful because they can be used to assess the effectiveness of criminal justice initiatives such as the **Anti-Social Behaviour Order (ASBO)** or an increase in the recruitment of police officers. A significant rise or fall in the statistics may indicate the success or failure of a particular **social policy**.

Trends in crime

Robert Reiner suggests that there are three distinct periods regarding trends in criminal behaviour, as follows.

Period 1: late 1950s to early 1980s – rapid rise in recorded crime

Until 1983, crime was measured using only those crimes reported to and recorded by the police. During this period, the OCS suggested that there was a dramatic rise in the volume of recorded crime in the UK and that all major categories of crime had substantial increases.

Types of crimes	1971	1984
Violence against the person (e.g. murder)	47 000	114 000
Sexual offences (e.g. rape and indecent assault)	23 000	20 000
Burglary	451 000	897 000
Robbery (e.g. armed robbery and mugging)	7 500	25 000
Theft and handling stolen goods (e.g. shoplifting and car theft)	1 003 000	1 808 000
Fraud and forgery	99 800	126 000

Table 1
Change in types of crimes from 1971–1984

Period 2: 1984 to 1993 – crime explosion

Between 1984 and 1993 the number of crimes that were recorded by the police increased by 111%. The number of crimes reported in the BCS, which was used alongside the OCS after 1983, rose by 77% during the same period.

Types of crimes	1984	1993
Violence against the person	114 000	205 000
Property crime	3 325 000	5 191 000
Vehicle offences	750 000	1 523 000

Table 2
Change in types of crimes from 1984–93

Period 3: 1994 to 2009 – falling crime, rising fear

Between 1994 and 2009, the crime rate fell significantly, in both the crimes recorded by the police and those reported to the BCS.

Types of crimes	1994	2009
Violence against the person	218 000	872 000
Property crime	4 895 000	3 032 000
Vehicle offences	1 384 000	495 000

Table 3
Change in types of crimes between 1994–2009

Despite the overall fall in crime, during the last 25 years recorded violence has increased as a proportion of all crime. In 1997, violent crime made up only 8% of all crime, but in 2009 violence accounted for 21% of all reported and recorded crime.

However, we need to make four important observations:

1. During 1998–99, the counting rules for crime used by the police changed significantly. In 2002 the National Crime Recording Standard (NCRS) was introduced. These changes resulted in the introduction of new offences, especially for less serious violent crime, and led to a steep rise in violence statistics.
2. The amount of violence reported to the BCS has declined. Since 1995, the number of violent incidents reported to the BCS has halved (50%) and is now at a similar level to that in 1981. This drop represents two million fewer incidents and about 800 000 fewer victims in 2009–10 compared to 1995.
3. Many types of serious violence, for example, manslaughter, murder, aggravated and grievous bodily harm and the use of guns and knives, have actually declined since the 1980s. However, in 2009, serious sexual crime increased by 7% compared to 2008.
4. As a proportion of all crime, violent crime has increased during the past 10 years because property crime has steeply declined since the mid-1990s.

Interpretivist sociologists suggest that the ways in which criminal statistics are collected and socially constructed are unreliable, so the picture of crime offered by the OCS does not reflect the reality of crime.

Examiners' notes

Official statistics regarding crime and other sociological issues (for example, education and suicide) are an important source of **secondary data** for sociologists. It is likely that in Section 2 of the exam paper, you will be asked questions on the merits of official statistics in a crime context. Make sure you know four to five general strengths of official statistics from a positivist perspective, four to five weaknesses from an interpretivist perspective and can adapt these to a crime and deviance context.

Essential notes

Young people may commit a range of crimes, but a group of crimes collectively known as **juvenile delinquency** have been singled out by some sociologists. Young people may commit these crimes, which generally do not involve financial reward, because of boredom, a search for excitement and, sometimes, malice. The crimes, usually committed by **subcultures** or gangs, include joy-riding, tagging, anti-social behaviour such as harassing members of the community, hooliganism, vandalism, territorial gang violence and drug-taking.

Distribution of crime and deviance by social group

An examination of statistics relating to police stops and arrests, convictions in the courts and the prison population suggests that some social groups tend to be more criminal than others.

Age

Approximately 50% of all crimes are committed by young people – statistical evidence shows that the older a person gets, the less likely he or she is to commit a crime. Most burglary, street robbery, violence against the person, shoplifting and criminal damage is committed by young people aged 17–24. The peak age for known male offenders is 18, compared to 15 for females.

Gender

About 80% to 90% of offenders found guilty or cautioned are male. As a result, male crime is said to outnumber female crime by an approximate ratio of 5 to 1. At least one-third of men are likely to be convicted for a criminal offence, compared to only 8% of women.

It has been found that men and women are convicted for different types of offences. For example, males dominate all offences but female conviction is likely to be for theft, particularly shoplifting. However, in recent years there has been a rapid rise in violence committed by young women (although it is still vastly outnumbered by male violent offences).

The following graph shows the relationships between age, gender and crime.

Fig 1
Offenders as a percentage of the population: by age
(2006, England and Wales)

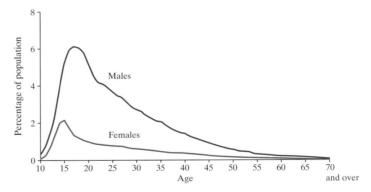

Essential notes

It is important to understand that most theories of crime are aimed at explaining male criminality. Some feminist sociologists argue that this 'malestream' criminology reflects **patriarchal** inequality. However, it also reflects the reality that, in 2008, there were 4 474 women in prison out of a total prison population of more than 83 000 – a mere 5.4%.

Ethnicity

Prison statistics show an over-representation of African-Caribbean men and women in prison – about one-tenth of male prisoners and one-fifth of female prisoners in UK prisons are African-Caribbean – yet this ethnic minority group makes up only 2.2% of the population. Police are more likely to **stop and search** black people than other groups. Black youths are more likely to be cautioned or given an ASBO than any other ethnic minority group. There has been a rise in the number of Asians who are arrested and convicted but their numbers are still below the national average.

The following table summarizes some of the patterns in the relationship between ethnicity and crime.

	Ethnicity						Total
	White	Mixed	Black	Asian	Chinese or Other	Not stated/ Unknown	
General population aged 10 & over (2001 **census**)	91.3	1.3	2.2	4.4	0.9	0.0	100
Stop and searches[1]	68.1	2.5	13.1	8.1	1.2	7.0	100
Arrests[2]	79.3	2.8	7.4	5.1	1.4	4.0	100
Cautions[2][3]	82.5		6.5	4.6	1.4	5.0	100
Youth offences	84.8	3.5	5.8	3.0	0.4	2.5	100
Tried at Crown Court[3][4]	73.5		14.0	8.0	4.4		100
Court ordered supervision by probation service[5]	83.6	2.5	6.3	4.6	1.2	1.8	100
Prison receptions[6]	79.1	2.9	10.6	5.9	1.2	0.2	100

Table 4
Percentage of ethnic groups at different stages of the criminal justice process compared to the ethnic breakdown of the general population, England and Wales 2007–08

Note:
Figures may not add up to 100% due to rounding.

[1] Stop and searches recorded by the police under section 1 of the Police and Criminal Evidence Act 1984 and other legislation.
[2] Notifiable offences.
[3] The data in these rows is based on ethnic appearance, and as such does not include the category Mixed ethnicity (the data in the rest of the table is based on self-identified ethnicity).
[4] Information on ethnicity is missing in 19% of cases; therefore, percentages are based on known ethnicity.
[5] Commencements.
[6] Sentenced.

Locality

Urban areas, especially inner-city areas and council estates, have higher rates of crime than suburbs or rural areas. (Refer to the following bar chart.) Therefore, inner-city and council estate residents (the urban poor), especially the elderly, are more likely than other social groups to be the victims of crime.

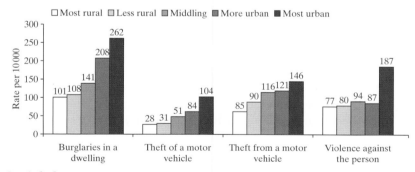

□ Most rural ▨ Less rural ▨ Middling ■ More urban ■ Most urban

Burglaries in a dwelling: 101 108 141 208 262
Theft of a motor vehicle: 28 31 51 84 104
Theft from a motor vehicle: 85 90 116 121 146
Violence against the person: 77 80 94 87 187

Rate per 10000

Fig 2
Recorded crime rates per 10 000 population by area type (2000–01)

Examiners' notes

All the factors – age, gender, ethnicity, locality and social class – may prompt essay questions that require you to explain why certain groups seem to commit more crime than others. Be aware that you can combine some of these factors. For example, female criminality is more likely to be committed by working-class girls, whereas most black teenagers who commit crime in inner-city areas come from deprived backgrounds.

Social class

Robert Reiner notes that there is a working-class bias in the prison population. Prior to being imprisoned, 74% were either unemployed or employed at the lowest occupational levels. Ann Hagell and Tim Newburn's study of youth detention centres found that only 8% of persistent offenders came from middle-class backgrounds. Offences can also be differentiated by social class. Middle-class offenders tend to be associated with **white-collar crime**, fraud and tax evasion; working-class offenders are found guilty mainly of burglary and street crime.

Essential notes

The counting rules that all police forces in the UK have to use to categorize and count crimes are constantly changing, which makes it difficult to compare crimes today with 'similar' crimes in the past. Moreover, the government contributes to this difficulty by continually introducing new laws, and therefore new crimes.

Essential notes

The dark figure of crime is an important idea, which you should be able to describe in detail. Its existence was particularly highlighted by the BCS when it was found that respondents reported crimes to survey researchers, but not to the police. Recent BCS survey data suggests that the dark figure may be receding because the gap between crimes reported to the police and crimes reported to the BCS is at its narrowest since the BCS began.

The social construction of the official crime statistics

It is often assumed, particularly by the mass media, that the official crime statistics (OCS) are **reliable** and valid in the picture of crime and criminality that they present. However, interpretivist sociologists (see p 48) argue that the OCS are of limited usefulness, are in fact a **social construction** and tell us more about the social groups involved in their collection – the general public, victims, the mass media, the police and the courts – than they tell us about crime and criminals.

Interpretivists point out that the OCS do not account for all the crime committed in the UK. They account only for those crimes that are recognized as such by victims and by the police. Sociologists have long argued that there exists a **dark figure** (sometimes referred to as the 'hidden iceberg') of unrecorded crime. It may be that the social characteristics of those who are not reported or caught may differ from those who are.

The existence of this dark figure of crime can be illustrated in various ways:

- Some criminal offences are not included in the OCS such as tax and VAT fraud or health and safety infringements. These offences are more likely to be committed by individuals who are wealthy and powerful.
- The police may exercise discretion in terms of how they define and consequently count crime because of political pressures to improve their clear-up rates or to improve efficiency. Crimes may be redefined by the police as 'less serious', for example, attempted burglary. Car theft may be defined as 'criminal damage'. Some crimes may not be recorded because the police regard them as too trivial to classify.
- Some offenders may belong to institutions such as the armed services, which police and punish criminals outside of the legal system. Public and state schools, professional associations such as the British Medical Association (BMA) and the Law Society, and financial institutions such as banks, prefer not to involve the police and courts because of the bad publicity that may be generated for their institutions. For example, schools may expel or suspend students for criminal activity such as vandalism and drugs, rather than involve the police. Therefore, these crimes will not be part of the OCS.
- There is evidence from the British Crime Survey (BCS) that many people, especially ethnic minorities, do not report crime because they have little faith in the police.
- Some victims may not be aware that a crime has been committed against them. An example is child abuse, which provides inaccurate statistics for exactly this reason.
- Some victims may fear humiliation at the hands of the police, the courts, the media and society in general, and so will be reluctant to report crime against them to the authorities. Rape, in particular, is thought to be greatly under-estimated by the OCS because of this.

The general public and victims of crime

Andy Pilkington argues that the OCS may not be useful because these statistics only tell us about the increased reporting of particular crimes by the general public and victims of crime, rather than actual increases in crime itself. For example:

- The general public has grown more intolerant of property crime as it has become more prosperous and **materialistic**. This has led to a greater public willingness to report theft and burglary. Increased affluence has also led to more people taking out insurance, which encourages reporting of property crime and criminal damage by victims.
- The OCS for some juvenile crimes may simply reflect public intolerance, fuelled by journalists' construction of **moral panics** in search of newsworthy stories – those guaranteed to sell newspapers or attract large television audiences. Moral panics increase the profile of the **folk devils** – groups regarded as a bad influence on society – so that the general public is more likely to recognize the problem and report it. This puts the police under pressure to curb the problem, which may lead to more arrests and prosecutions. The government may pass new laws in order to control the so-called problem. The folk devil group may react by becoming more confrontational and criminal. In other words, the moral panic leads to **deviancy amplification** – an artificial rise in criminal statistics (see p 42).
- Some crimes such as soft drug offences, homosexual importuning and prostitution appear to have no victim, and therefore may not be reported by the general public as consistently as other crimes. These victimless crimes depend on police detection. Such detection varies from area to area. Some police forces may ignore prostitution or soft drug use, whereas others may frequently crack down on these offences. As a result, it is often difficult for sociologists to trust or compare the statistics relating to these crimes.

When taking these factors into consideration, criminologists have estimated that for every 100 crimes committed, 47 will be reported to the police, 27 will be recorded by the police, and five will be cleared up in the form of a caution or conviction. **Self-report studies** indicate that the volume of crime should be greater and that females and middle-class males are just as likely to commit a crime as those included in the crime statistics.

Essential notes

A big problem for sociologists when examining the OCS is that the 43 police forces in the UK do not police in a standardized way. They enjoy considerable discretion in how they police the law, which makes it difficult to compare like with like.

Examiners' notes

Questions about the merits of self-report studies often appear in Section 2 of the exam paper, so you need to be aware of the arguments for and against them as a source of information about crime.

The police

Interpretivists argue that the OCS tell us more about the nature of policing in the UK than about crime and criminality. In particular, they may tell us a great deal about how police officers interact with suspects, especially those from relatively powerless social groups. Therefore, interpretivists question the validity of the picture of criminality that the OCS provides. They suggest that young, working-class and African-Caribbean people frequently appear in these statistics because they are profiled and targeted by the police rather than because they are more criminal. This can be illustrated in several ways:

- Studies of police officers on patrol conducted by Joan Smith, Christopher Grey and Aaron Cicourel indicate that they operate using stereotypical assumptions or labels about what constitutes 'suspicious' or 'criminal' behaviour; that is, the decision to stop or arrest someone may be based on whether they correspond to a **stereotype.**

- There is strong evidence from Simon Holdaway, Ben Bowling, Coretta Phillips and the MacPherson Report that suggests racial profiling by some police officers may be a crucial element governing their decision to stop African-Caribbeans. Statistics released in 2010 show that police stop and search African-Caribbeans six times more often and Asians twice as often as they do white people. Sociological studies of the occupational or **canteen culture** of the police suggest that it sustains racist attitudes among some rank and file police officers. Holdaway found that older and more experienced officers use racist language as a matter of course in the presence of younger officers, while Bowling and Phillips noted that some police officers in London based their decision to stop young black males in cars on a stereotype known as 'driving while black'. Police officers assumed that black youths were driving upmarket cars because either they were drug dealers or they had stolen them. John Lea and Jock Young also note a military-style police presence in ethnic-minority-dominated areas, which may result in more confrontation between police and young black people which artificially amplifies the OCS.

- Holdaway notes that, in general, young people – particularly those from working-class backgrounds – are more likely to fit police stereotypes about criminality than older or middle-class people. These stereotypes are likely to lead to a greater police presence in some urban neighbourhoods.

- Feminist criminologists argue that male officers tend to adopt **paternalistic** attitudes towards female offenders, who are less likely to be stopped, arrested and charged. For example, when caught committing criminal offences, they are more likely to be cautioned than arrested and charged. Pollack calls this the **chivalry factor**. According to Ministry of Justice statistics in 2007, 49% of female offenders received a caution. Only 30% of male offenders received the same. Research also indicates that police culture is very masculine (fewer than 20% of police officers are women) and interaction with men or ethnic minorities may be shaped by a need to be seen by other officers as being tough.

The courts

There is evidence that juries and judges also engage in stereotyping. It has been found that middle-class offenders and women are much more likely to be found not guilty by juries. When they are found guilty, they are treated more leniently by an upper-class male-dominated judiciary. Roger Hood's observations of criminal courts found that even when black youths were up for the same offence as white youths, they were 17% more likely to get a prison sentence. The OCS may therefore tell us more about judicial attitudes than about crime and criminality.

The Marxist critique of the OCS

Marxists are also very critical of the OCS. They suggest that the capitalist state collects and constructs criminal statistics in order to serve the interests of the ruling class. The statistics serve an **ideological function** – whoever has the power to collect and construct such statistics has the power to control and manipulate public opinion. Therefore, Marxists argue that the ideological function of the OCS is to criminalize groups such as the young, the working class and African-Caribbeans. This divides and rules the working class by diverting white conformist working-class attention away from class inequalities.

Furthermore, Steven Box argues that the OCS divert attention from both middle-class white-collar and **corporate crime**. Box argues that crimes committed by the powerful are not pursued as vigorously or punished as harshly as working-class crimes. He also argues that the powerful engage in anti-social activities, which result in death, injury and theft for ordinary people but are often not defined as criminal because the ruling class constructs laws to reflect their own interests.

However, in contrast, Left Realists such as Jock Young and John Lea (see p 24) note that the Islington crime survey data suggests that the OCS are largely correct and that young working-class people and, depending on the area, African-Caribbean people do commit more crime than other social groups despite the influence of moral panics, police stereotyping and judicial bias.

Examiners' notes

It is important to group arguments for and against the OCS into theoretical categories. Most arguments in favour of the use of statistics are positivist. Interpretivists are generally critical of the ways in which statistics are collected. However, do not neglect the Marxist position, as it gives insight into why few middle-class crimes are included in the official picture of crime.

Functionalist explanations of crime and deviance

Functionalists argue that crime and deviance can only be explained by looking at the way societies are organized socially – their **social structures** – and that crime is caused by society rather than by the circumstances of the individual. Functionalism is therefore a **structuralist theory** of crime.

Émile Durkheim

Émile Durkheim believed that in pre-industrial societies, crime was rare because family and religion were powerful agencies of socialization and **social control**. This ensured an influential combination of **consensus** and community, which exercised a powerful influence over personal behaviour. Durkheim also believed that crime rates were higher in cities, as the complexity of modern life undermined the authority of religion and family. Consensus, community and social controls are weaker, so people are more likely to experience **anomie** – a sense of moral confusion that weakens their commitment to shared values and rules, encouraging crime and deviance.

Durkheim observed that crime and deviance were present in all societies. He speculated that crime **functions** for the benefit of society in these ways:

- Acts of crime and deviance can provoke positive social change by highlighting aspects of the social structure or law that are inadequate. For example, the Suffragette movement broke the law in order to highlight gender inequalities.
- Some crimes such as terrorist attacks create public outrage, which reinforces community solidarity against the offenders.
- Pursuit, trial and punishment of criminals reassures people that society is functioning effectively, while reminding them of acceptable social boundaries of behaviour.
- Minor crimes can act as safety valves, preventing more serious crimes.

Evaluation of Durkheim

- He never explains why certain social groups commit crime.
- He neglects the fact that some crimes are always **dysfunctional**.
- Marxists argue that he underestimates the level of conflict and inequality in modern societies.

Robert Merton

Robert Merton argued that the cause of crime lies in the relationship between the culture and the social structure of society. In capitalist societies, cultural institutions such as the mass media socialize individuals into believing that material success is a realistic goal.

However, Merton notes that resources and opportunities are not fairly distributed in capitalist societies. Those at the bottom of society may experience a **strain** between their goals and the legitimate institutional means (education and work), as the chance of accessing these is blocked by those with economic and social advantages. This can produce anomie, which, Merton argued, individuals could respond to in various ways:

Response	Method of individual's response
Conformity	Most of the population cope by doing their best and making the most of what society offers them
Innovation	Commitment to cultural goals may remain strong, but some people reject the conventional means of acquiring wealth and turn to illegal means
Ritualism	Some people have lost sight of material goals, but derive satisfaction from fairly meaningless jobs
Retreatism	A small number of people reject both the goals and the means, by dropping out of society
Rebellion	People may rebel and seek to replace shared goals and institutional means with more radical alternatives, and may use violent methods to achieve this

Merton concludes that criminals are not that different from law-abiding citizens. They have the same goals – to achieve material success.

Evaluation of Merton

- Merton does not explain why some individuals commit crime, yet others conform, retreat or rebel.
- Merton's theory explains crime that results in economic gain, but he does not explain many forms of violent and sexual crimes.
- He also fails to explain crimes committed by young people in gangs, which do not seem to be motivated by material goals.
- White-collar and corporate crime arise from access to opportunities rather than the blocking of them.
- Merton fails to ask who benefits from the capitalist system and especially the laws that underpin it. Marxists, like Steven Box, suggest that the ruling capitalist class benefits most from the way laws are currently organized.

However, Sumner claims that Merton has uncovered the main cause of crime in modern societies – the alienation caused by disillusionment with the impossible goals set by **capitalism**.

Key study

Jock Young is a sociologist and criminologist. His work, *The Vertigo of Late Modernity* (2009), is very influenced by Merton's ideas.

Young argues that key institutions in the UK such as educational establishments and the media stress the **meritocratic** ideal. He also argues that meritocracy is a myth and that a 'chaos of inequality' characterizes financial rewards in the UK – business leaders and celebrities are paid huge sums of money, yet hard-working people in full-time jobs struggle to survive. Young argues that there is a contradiction between culture, which focuses on monetary success and acquiring material goods, and the institutions that make up the social structure, which fail to deliver material success for most people. He notes that this contradiction produces anomie and much violent criminality is a response to this.

Essential notes

Think about how a sociologist might research the validity of Merton's ideas. What sample of people could be used to research whether people are suffering from anomie and adopting these responses? What method might a positivist sociologist prefer, compared with an interpretivist researcher?

Table 5
Responses to anomie

Examiners' notes

Successful evaluation is balanced evaluation – it should contain reference to the strengths as well as the weaknesses of particular studies or theories.

Essential notes

Be aware of the other theories that Merton influenced, especially Cohen's subcultural theory, Cloward and Ohlin's theory of illegitimate opportunity structure and Cashmore's theory as to why black youths might commit crime (see pp 14–15, 33–34).

Subcultural explanations of crime and deviance

Subcultural theory focuses on explaining why young working-class people commit crime. Known as juvenile delinquency, it is often malicious in nature and not linked to material or financial goals. Subcultural theory also tries to explain why juvenile delinquency has a collective or subcultural character – it is committed as part of a larger group or gang.

Albert Cohen

Albert Cohen, like Merton, argues that delinquency is caused by a strain between cultural goals and the institutional means of achieving them. He suggests that young people want status, respect and to feel valued. Middle-class youngsters usually attain these things from their parents, teachers and peers as they achieve educational success.

However, Cohen suggests that working-class boys are denied status at school, as their parents have failed to equip them with the skills they need. Thus, these boys are placed in the bottom sets and consequently are unable to acquire the knowledge and status enjoyed by students in the higher sets. Such boys may leave school with few or no qualifications and then work in low-paid jobs or are unemployed. In this sense, they are denied status by wider society.

Cohen argues that these experiences result in low self-esteem. These boys feel alienated and angry at the low status that schools and society allocate them. They experience a form of anomie, called '**status frustration**' by Cohen. They respond by developing gangs or subcultures of like-minded boys who reverse the norms and values of the dominant culture and award one another status on the basis of anti-school and delinquent behaviour.

Evaluation of Cohen

- Paul Willis concludes that the working-class youths in Cohen's study of working-class underachievement did not share the same definition of status as middle-class boys. They defined educational failure as 'success' because qualifications were not necessary for the types of factory jobs they wanted.
- Most working-class boys actually conform at school despite educational failure.
- Cohen ignores female delinquency.
- He neglects the role of agencies of social control in the social construction of delinquency. For example, police stereotyping of working-class youths might mean they are more likely to be stopped and searched.

Walter Miller

Walter Miller argues that working-class juvenile delinquents are merely acting out and exaggerating the mainstream values of working-class subculture. Miller suggests that working-class youth subculture has developed a series of '**focal concerns**', which give meaning to their lives outside work. These include a heightened sense of masculinity – which sees violence as an acceptable problem-solving device – a desire for excitement and being anti-authority. Living out these focal concerns compensates for the boredom of school and factory jobs. However, it may also cause confrontation with teachers and the police. Thus, Miller blames working-class delinquency on what he sees as the potentially deviant nature of working-class culture.

Richard Cloward and Lloyd Ohlin

Richard Cloward and Lloyd Ohlin argue that the type of crime committed by young people depends on the type of **illegitimate opportunity structure** that is available to them in their area. They identify three illegitimate opportunity structures that produce three types of subcultures:

1. In some areas, there are established patterns of illegitimate opportunity in which people experience criminal 'careers'. These organized types of criminal subcultures mirror legitimate businesses, in that employees have specific roles and can be promoted upwards to managerial or executive status. Sudhir Venkatesh observed such a subculture in Chicago in his study *Gang Leader for a Day*.
2. Some inner-city areas may be dominated by conflict subcultures, which engage in highly masculinized territorial or respect-driven violence. Pitts found that local youth in inner-city London found it difficult to resist gang membership because the risk to themselves and their families from non-affiliation was too great.
3. If young people fail to gain access to either the criminal or conflict subcultures, they may form retreatist subcultures, in which the major activities are drug use, and commit crimes such as burglary and shoplifting to finance it.

Criticisms of subcultural theory

David Matza, an interactionist sociologist, suggests that subcultural theories have the following problems:

- Most young working-class people experience status frustration but do not become delinquents.
- Only a minority of youth actually become delinquents.
- Some young people drift in and out of delinquency, but eventually grow out of it when they reach adulthood.
- When justifying or explaining their delinquency, young people rarely make reference to membership of subcultures.
- Subcultural theories generally neglect the role of the police, who may target young working-class people as potentially criminal and frequently stop, search and arrest them, whereas they ignore similar behaviour in high-status groups.

Essential notes

Although Miller's theory is subcultural, it bears little resemblance to Cohen's theory, which partly blames society for gang activity. Miller strongly implies that working-class culture is problematic and inferior compared to middle-class culture. His theory is not dissimilar to the 'underclass' theory of Charles Murray.

Examiners' notes

Venkatesh's study is a good example of **participant observation**. Study it in some detail so that you can clearly recognize the strengths and limitations of this research method in the study of gangs. Compare it with UK research into gangs that has used participant observation, especially James Patrick's *A Glasgow Street Gang Observed*, which used a covert form of participant observation.

Essential notes

Most interactionists believe that crime and deviance are a social construction – the end product of decisions made by the powerful. Young or working-class people appear in the criminal statistics frequently. Though their behaviour is more likely to be defined as problematic, they are targeted by the police. In other words, subcultural theories aim to explain why young working-class people commit crime because the official crime statistics (OCS) say they do, yet these statistics may not be valid.

Ecological explanations of crime and deviance

The official crime statistics (OCS) show that recorded crime is not evenly distributed between geographical areas. It is higher in urban areas than in rural areas, and higher in inner cities and on council estates compared to suburban areas of cities and towns (see p 7). British Crime Survey (BCS) data suggests that people who live in rural areas worry less about crime than city residents. Urban dwellers are also more likely to perceive their areas as experiencing high levels of anti-social behaviour.

Some theories have therefore examined the environment or **ecology** of towns and cities in order to explain crime. During the 1920s, the Chicago School of sociologists looked at the relationship between criminality and the urban environment, and attempted to explain why crime rates were so high in cities.

Clifford Shaw and Henry McKay, who examined the organization of American cities such as Chicago, observed that most are arranged into distinct neighbourhoods or zones, each with its own distinctive subcultural values and lifestyles. Shaw and McKay paid particular attention to 'zone two', the inner city, naming it the **zone of transition**. It was characterized by cheap rented housing, poverty, high numbers of immigrants and high crime rates. They noted that 'relative' crime rates in the inner city were similar over a number of years, even though the immigrant groups dominating the zone had changed. This indicated that the high crime rates were not due to the specific cultural characteristics of specific immigrant groups.

Shaw and McKay concluded that the constant movement of people in and out of these areas prevented the formation of stable communities and a sense of social control. Instead, it produced a state of **social disorganization**, with little sense of community. As a result, people were unlikely to feel a sense of duty and obligation to one another, and so felt little guilt about committing crimes against their neighbours. This theory, which is influenced by Durkheim's theory of anomie, therefore links rising crime rates to the decline of community.

Shaw and McKay note that areas of social disorganization produce subcultures of delinquency, which culturally transmit criminal behaviour, skills and values from one generation to the next. This **cultural transmission** ensures that young criminals, whether male or female, learn criminal skills and traditions from the older generation, and that social disorganization is reproduced and maintained. Edwin Sutherland's idea of '**differential association**' is a very similar concept. He suggests that cultural behaviour is shaped by those around them. If people who live in a socially disorganized urban area frequently associate with people who make their living from crime, then the choice to pursue a criminal career may not be a difficult option.

Gordon Marshall *et al.* suggest that zones of transition made up of sink estates and deteriorating inner-city areas can be spotted in UK cities. They argue that these areas lack any sense of community spirit or social control. As a result, some people feel free to commit crime at will. Such disorganization is reinforced by the state's failure to address **social problems** such as unemployment, poverty, poor mental health, and drug and alcohol abuse.

Evaluation of ecological explanations

- Shaw and McKay's analysis of crime is tautological, meaning that it is unclear which comes first, the crime or the social disorganization. For example, social disorganization might be the effect of high crime rates rather than the cause of them.
- The majority of people living in areas with high crime rates choose not to commit crime despite being stereotyped by Shaw and McKay's theory. However, although children and teenagers may sometimes be involved in delinquency, the evidence suggests that there is very little adolescent commitment to the notion of gangs or subcultures in most urban areas and that involvement for most is either non-existent or fleeting, which means that they might drift in and out on the fringes of these subcultures. This challenges the concepts of cultural transmission and differential association.
- The ecological approach neglects the fact that evidence for inner-city crime tends to come from the OCS, which are socially constructed and may tell sociologists more about policing than about crime and criminals. For example, the disproportionate amount of urban crime found in the OCS may be due to the military-style over-policing of these areas and the excessive use of stop and search.
- John Baldwin and A. E. Bottoms blame **tipping** – the way local people interpret social changes in their area – for urban decline. If law-abiding people perceive their area to be changing for the worse because of anti-social behaviour, they may move out and be replaced by the friends and relatives of those responsible for the anti-social behaviour. If the anti-social families outweigh the respectable families, the area has tipped and will be regarded by the police, local council and the community as a 'problem'.

Essential notes

This critique of the ecological approach comes from an interpretivist perspective and suggests that some groups appear more in the OCS because those with power are able to label them as criminals.

Key study

Dick Hobbs *et al.* identify what they call a **night-time economy**.

They found that since the 1990s the number of clubs and pubs in city centres has grown rapidly, catering primarily for the leisure needs of younger people. Vast numbers of young people come to city centres within a very narrow time frame to seek pleasure through drinking and socializing.

Later research by Hobbs *et al.* illustrates this point. In Manchester, around 75 000 people are out on Friday and Saturday nights and about 75% of all violent incidents in urban areas occur at the weekend between 9 pm and 3 am, often fuelled by drink and drugs. There are only about 30 police officers to control the 'night-time economy' in Manchester. The main responsibility for social control has passed to private security companies in the form of door staff or 'bouncers'.

Examiners' notes

Like functionalism and feminism, Marxism is also a structural theory, which believes that the organization or structure of capitalist society shapes people's behaviour. You need to know the Marxist theory of society, especially the relationship between **infrastructure** and **superstructure**, and be able to illustrate this using material from your study of the family, education, religion and crime – the Theory and Method exam question may focus on this.

Examiners' notes

It is a good idea to be aware of contemporary examples from the news that you can use to illustrate these ideas. For example, in 2010 there was controversy over Vodafone's tax bill. Using examples is a good way to convince the examiner that you understand the debate.

Marxist explanations of crime and deviance

Marxists argue that the nature and organization of capitalism creates the potential for criminal behaviour. This can be illustrated in two ways.

1. David Gordon argues that capitalism is characterized by class inequalities in the distribution of, for example, wealth and income, poverty, unemployment and homelessness. He suggests that most working-class crime is a realistic and rational response to these inequalities. Gordon argues that, considering the nature of capitalism, we should not ask 'why the working class commit crime' but instead 'why they don't commit more crime'.

2. Gordon argues that the **ideology** of capitalism encourages criminal behaviour in all social classes; for example, values such as competition, materialism and consumerism as well as the profit motive encourage a culture of greed and self-interest. The need to win at all costs or go out of business as well as the desire for self-enrichment encourage capitalists to commit white-collar and corporate crimes such as tax evasion. Capitalism also encourages a 'culture of envy' among poorer sections of society that may also encourage a criminal reaction.

The law as ideology and social control

Marxists, like Louis Althusser, argue that the law is an **ideological state apparatus**, which functions in the interests of the capitalist class to maintain and legitimate class inequality in the following ways:

- It is concerned mainly with protecting the major priorities of capitalism – wealth, private property and profit. Laureen Snider notes that the capitalist state is reluctant to pass laws that regulate the activities of businesses or threaten their profitability.
- Box notes that the powerful kill, injure, maim and steal from ordinary members of society but these killings, injuries and thefts are often not covered by the law. For example, a worker's death due to employer infringements of health and safety laws is a civil, rather than criminal offence.
- Law enforcement is selective and tends to favour the rich and powerful. For example, social security fraud, largely committed by the poor, inevitably attracts prosecution and often prison, yet tax fraudsters, who are usually wealthy and powerful individuals rather than ordinary taxpayers, rarely get taken to court.
- Jeffrey Reiman (2001) argues that the more likely a crime is to be committed by higher-class people, the less likely it is to be treated as a criminal offence. In particular, white-collar and corporate crimes are under-policed and under-punished.

White-collar and corporate crime

Hazel Croall defines white-collar crime as crime committed in the course of legitimate employment, which involves the abuse of an occupational role. Croall suggests fraud, accounting offences, tax evasion, insider dealing and computer crime as being typical white-collar crimes. Croall notes that people who own the means of production or who manage them have greater opportunities than most to make large sums of money from crime.

Croall notes that companies also commit crimes, known as corporate crimes. Examples are:

Type of crime	Example
Crimes against consumers	Manufacturing and selling dangerous goods or foods; not ensuring the safety of passengers
Crimes against employees	In the UK, between 1965 and 1995, 25 000 people were killed in the workplace; about 70% of these deaths were due to employer violation of health and safety laws
Environmental offences	Pollution
Financial fraud	False accounting; share price fixing

Croall argues that despite the fact that the costs of corporate and white-collar crimes far outstrip the overall combined annual value of burglary, theft and robbery, they are not regarded as a serious problem by the general public for the following reasons:

- These offences are often invisible and hidden from the public gaze. People do not fear white-collar or corporate crime in the same way as they do robbery or violence.
- Many of these crimes are complex, as they involve the abuse of technical, financial or scientific knowledge.
- Responsibility is often delegated or diffused in companies, so it may be difficult to decide where blame lies.
- Victimization tends to be indirect – offenders and victims rarely come face-to-face, and many people may not realize that they have been victims of a crime.
- Croall notes that there is often a very fine line between what are morally acceptable and unacceptable business practices.
- Many of the regulatory bodies, which monitor these types of crimes, advise and warn offenders rather than punish them. Corporate offenders are rarely taken to court.

Evaluation of traditional Marxism

- It largely ignores the relationship between crime and important non-class variables such as ethnicity and gender.
- Not all poor people commit crime, despite the pressures of living in poverty in a money-obsessed society.
- The criminal justice system sometimes acts against the interests of the capitalist class.

Essential notes

Marxists argue that capitalism is criminogenic – this means that it is a natural outcome of capitalist practices and values.

Table 6
Examples of corporate crimes

Essential notes

Think about how you would explain why people who are already rich and powerful might be motivated to commit crimes. The ideas of Gordon, **functionalists** and Left Realists might help.

Examiners' notes

White-collar and corporate crime is a difficult subject to research because of its nature and the fact that its perpetrators have the power to deny sociologists access to, for example, their offices, companies and staff. Primary research could be focused on the victims of specific types of white-collar or corporate crimes, but many sociologists working in this field are dependent on secondary sources. What secondary data might a sociologist use to investigate white-collar or corporate crime, and what are their strengths and limitations?

Neo-Marxist explanations of crime and deviance – the 'New Criminology'

Neo-Marxists are sociologists who have been influenced by many of the ideas of traditional Marxism, which they combine with ideas from other approaches, such as **labelling theory**.

The 'New Criminology' of Ian Taylor, Paul Walton and Jock Young is the most well-known example of **Neo-Marxism**. This generally agrees with the traditional Marxist analysis that:

- Capitalist society is based on exploitation and class conflict and characterized by extreme inequalities of wealth and power.
- The state makes and enforces laws in the interests of the capitalist class and criminalizes members of the working class.

However, Neo-Marxists are critical of traditional Marxism, which they argue is too deterministic. For example:

Traditional Marxists	See the working class as the passive victims of capitalism, who are driven to criminality by factors beyond their control
Neo-Marxists	Reject the ideas of the traditional Marxists. Instead, they are '**voluntarists**', which means they believe that individuals have free will. They argue that the working class and members of ethnic minority groups experience the constraints of capitalism and then make choices about how they should react to this experience

From a Neo-Marxist perspective, crime is a deliberate and meaningful political response by the powerless to their position within the capitalist system. The poor and the powerless commit crime as a way of protesting against injustice, exploitation and alienation. Neo-Marxists claim that crimes against property, such as theft and burglary, are a reaction to wealth inequality. Vandalism is a symbolic attack on society's obsession with property. Criminals are therefore not the passive victims of capitalism – they are actively struggling to alter capitalism and to change society for the better.

Neo-Marxists argue that the ruling class is aware of the revolutionary potential of working-class crime and has taken steps to control it – state apparatuses such as the police target working-class areas, while the state has introduced 'repressive' laws such as the Criminal Justice Acts to control the 'problem' population. Stuart Hall claims that moral panics about potentially disruptive groups such as the young and ethnic minorities are often created by the mass media working on behalf of the state in order to divide and rule a potentially troublesome working class. Hall analysed how the tabloid media presented 'mugging' or street robbery in the 1970s as a new crime in which black criminals robbed white victims. He claims this had the ideological function of dividing the black and white working class and setting them against each other, thereby diverting attention from the mismanagement of capitalism in this period by the ruling class.

Examiners' notes

The Theory and Method exam question may ask you to compare structuralist approaches with social action theories. The New Criminology combines structuralist Marxism with aspects of **social action theory**, that is, the idea that people experience and interpret the world around them and make choices as to how they should react.

Table 7
Example of the difference between traditional Marxism and Neo-Marxism

Essential notes

The Neo-Marxist theory sees working-class criminals as politically motivated by their negative experience of capitalism. It presents criminals as 'Robin Hoods' – stealing from the rich and redistributing to the poor. Some sociologists, most notably Paul Gilroy, have suggested that young black criminals are politically motivated to commit crime by their discovery of the history of slavery and colonialism as well as by their experience of racism and police harassment.

Evaluation of the 'New Criminology'

- Left Realists (see p 24) have criticized the New Criminology for over-romanticizing working-class criminals as 'Robin Hoods' who are fighting capitalism by stealing from the rich and giving to the poor.
- The reality of crime is that most victims of working-class and black crime are themselves working class and black. It is suggested that Taylor *et al.* do not take the effects of this type of crime on working-class victims seriously.
- It is difficult to imagine a political motive underpinning crimes such as domestic violence, rape and child abuse.
- Roger Hopkins Burke (2005) concludes that Marxism and the 'New Criminology' is too general to explain crime and too idealistic to tackle it practically.

Marxist subcultural theory

Some Marxists have focused on working-class deviant or 'spectacular' youth subcultures, such as teddy boys (1950s), mods and rockers (1960s), skinheads (1970s), punks (late 1970s) and ravers (1980s/1990s). They suggest that these can be seen as a form of ideological resistance to the dominant adult value system shaped by middle-class and capitalist values.

Key study

The Birmingham Centre for Contemporary Cultural Studies (CCCS) argued that youth subcultural styles should be read as a challenge to the class inequality that characterizes capitalist society.

For example, Phil Cohen (1972) studied 1970s skinheads and proposed that the skinhead style was a symbolic reaction to the decline of working-class communities, whose dress exaggerated working-class masculinity and aggression, while their anti-immigrant stance was a reaction to the decline of their white working-class neighbourhoods.

Dick Hebdige (1979) looked for the meanings behind the style of punk rockers in the late 1970s. He argues that punks set out to deliberately shock the establishment and society by adopting a style that reused ordinary objects such as bin-liners and safety pins, as well as deviant symbols such as the swastika and sexual bondage gear, to symbolically resist the dominant cultural values of the UK society of the time.

However, Hebdige notes that capitalist society quickly adapts to such challenges to its cultural dominance. He notes that punks and other youth subcultures are fairly short-lived because of **incorporation** – capitalism quickly commercializes aspects of youth cultural style, that is, puts them on sale, and strips them of their ideological significance so that they become just another consumer item.

Evaluation of Marxist subcultural theory

- Marxists neglect gender and ethnicity as influences on youth subculture.
- They underestimate the extent to which changes in youth culture are created by capitalism and shaped by consumerism.
- **Globalization**, particularly in the form of American cultural influences, is neglected.

Essential notes

The concept of social construction is very important, as it suggests that those who are defined and labelled as criminals are the victims of those with power, who disapprove of their behaviour. This strongly implies that people who are labelled criminals or deviants are not responsible for their deviance – rather, that the label is the product of power inequalities.

Essential notes

Interactionists are very critical of the OCS, which they argue are also a social construction. They suggest that the OCS tell us more about the groups involved in their collection, especially victims, the police and the courts, than they tell us about crime and criminality.

Interactionist explanations of crime and deviance

Interactionist approaches to crime and deviance belong to the interpretivist tradition, which is interested in how people interpret and therefore socially construct the world around them. They are also interested in looking at how criminality develops in the social interactions between a potential deviant and agents of social control.

The relativity of deviance

Interactionists believe that 'normality' and 'deviance' are relative concepts because there is no universal or fixed agreement on how to define them. They point out that definitions of 'right' or 'wrong' behaviour differ according to social context. For example, nudity is fine in the privacy of the bathroom or bedroom but may be interpreted as a symptom of mental illness or criminality if persistently carried out in public.

Definitions of deviance change according to historical period; for example, homosexuality and suicide were defined as illegal activities until the 1960s. The definitions also change according to the cultural or subcultural context; for example, drinking alcohol is illegal in Saudi Arabia and disapproved of by Muslims in the UK.

The interpretation of deviance

Interactionists believe that deviance is therefore a matter of interpretation. For example, society generally disapproves of killing people, although killing in self-defence and in battle are interpreted as necessary actions by society.

The social construction of deviance

Howard Becker argues that there is no such thing as a deviant act because no act is inherently criminal or deviant in itself, in all situations and at all times. Instead, it becomes criminal or deviant only when others label it as such.

Becker therefore argues that the social construction of deviance requires two activities. One group, which normally lacks power, acts in a particular way. Another group, with more power, responds negatively to it and defines and labels it as criminal. Therefore, for Becker, a deviant is simply someone to whom a label has been successfully applied and deviant behaviour is simply behaviour that people have labelled as such.

Becker notes that powerful groups create rules or laws in order to define what counts as crime and deviance, and label those who fail to conform to these social controls as criminals or outlaws (outsiders).

The agents of social control

Becker notes that the agents of social control are made up of groups such as the police, the judiciary, social workers and probation workers. They work on behalf of politically powerful groups to label and thus define the behaviour of less powerful groups as being a problem. Consequently, the behaviour of the less powerful is subjected to greater surveillance and control by these social agencies.

Primary and secondary deviance

Edwin Lemert distinguishes between **primary deviance** and **secondary deviance**. Primary deviance refers to insignificant deviant acts that have not been publicly labelled. Such acts have little significance for a person's status or identity and, as a result, primary deviants do not see themselves as deviant.

Secondary deviance is the result of societal reaction – of labelling. Being caught and publicly labelled as a criminal can involve being **stigmatized**, shunned and excluded from normal society. The criminal label can become a **master status**, which means that society interprets all actions and motives in the context of the label. For example, if a person is labelled a 'sex offender', the label shapes people's reactions to any other status the person has.

Secondary deviance is likely to provoke further hostile reactions from society such as prejudice and discrimination. For example, ex-cons may find it difficult to find legitimate employment. This may lead to a **deviant career** – the practical consequences of treating a person as a deviant may produce a **self-fulfilling prophecy** in so much as the labelled person may see him- or herself as deviant and act accordingly.

The person labelled a deviant may consequently seek comfort, sympathy, normality and status in a subculture of other people branded with a similar label. This in turn creates the potential for further deviance.

Evaluation of labelling theory

- Labelling theory has shown that defining deviance is a complex rather than a simple process.
- It has shown that definitions of deviance are relative and therefore not fixed, universal or unchangeable.
- Labelling theory was the first theory to draw sociological attention to the consequences of being labelled a deviant.

However:

- Peter Ackers argues that the deviant act is always more important than the societal reaction to it. Deviants don't need to wait until a label is attached to understand that what they are doing or have done is or was wrong.
- Labelling theory fails to explain the origin of deviance – it does not explain why people commit deviance in the first place, before they are labelled.
- Labelling theory implies that once someone is labelled, a deviant career is inevitable.
- Left Realists argue that it is guilty of over-romanticizing deviance and blaming the agencies of social control for causing crime. This ignores the real victims of crime.

Essential notes

Interactionist studies of crime have focused on how certain groups have come to be labelled as deviant by agents of social control such as the police and the mass media, and how such groups have reacted to the negative labels that have been applied to them. For example, Simon Holdaway's **covert participant observation** (conducted when he was a serving police officer) clearly shows that police officers negatively label and treat particular groups, notably ethnic minorities, and that this stereotyping may be responsible for their disproportionate appearance in the OCS.

Essential notes

The concept of power is central to the interactionist analysis. However, Marxists are critical of this theory, because interactionists are vague about the source of this power. Marxists argue that the power to label groups as criminal or deviant arises from the organization of capitalist society.

Left Realist explanations of crime and deviance

The Left Realists John Lea and Jock Young aim to explain street crime committed by young people in urban areas. Their **victim (or victimization) survey** of inner-city London (the Islington Crime Survey) suggested that working-class and black people, especially elderly women, have a realistic fear of street crime, because they reported that they are often the victims of such crime.

Lea and Young's explanation of why working-class and African-Caribbean young people commit crime revolves around three key concepts:

1. Relative deprivation

This refers to how deprived someone feels in relation to others, or compared with their own expectations. **Relative deprivation** can lead to crime when people feel resentment that, unfairly, others are better off than them. Lea and Young note that although people today are more prosperous compared with the past, they are more aware of their relative deprivation because of media and advertising, which raise everyone's expectations about standards of living.

Left Realism argues that working class youth feel relatively deprived compared to middle class youth, while African-Caribbean youth compare themselves to white Britons with regard to life chances and opportunities such as living standards, access to consumer goods and income. These groups feel that they are relatively worse-off through no fault of their own. For example, young black Britons may feel that racism is holding them back.

Feelings of relative deprivation are heightened when combined with **individualism** – the pursuit of self-interest – and are likely to lead to criminal responses because individualism undermines the family and community values of mutual support, cooperation and selflessness. The informal social controls usually exercised by the family and community are weakened. As a result, anti-social behaviour, violence and crime increase.

2. Marginalization

Left Realists argue that young people often feel **marginalized** (they feel they have little or no power to change their situation) and frustrated – negative treatment by the police and the authorities may result in further feelings of hostility and resentment towards mainstream society which may spill over into confrontation with authority.

3. Subculture

Some young working-class and black people who experience these feelings of relative deprivation and marginalization may form deviant subcultures. These subcultures react to their perception that society does not value them, by becoming involved in street crimes such as drug pushing, territorial gang violence, anti-social behaviour, joy-riding and mugging.

Left Realist solutions to crime

Left Realists argue that the only way to cut crime is to:

Improve policing and control

Lea and Young argue that crime can only be reduced with the assistance of local communities. However, the military-style policing of inner-city communities, particularly black communities, has alienated local populations. For example, stop and search statistics in urban areas suggest that the police use racial profiling in their attempt to identify criminality, and this has led to accusations of **institutional racism**. Lea and Young argue that the police need to regain the confidence of local communities so that people feel comfortable providing them with information about crime.

Deal with the deeper structural causes of crime

The main cause of crime is the deeply unequal nature of capitalist society and its inequalities in income, wealth and opportunity, which have undermined social cohesion and produced a culture of envy, frustration and hostility. Lea and Young argue that crime can only be reduced or eliminated by improving people's opportunities to achieve a decent standard of living. This can only be done by reducing income and wealth inequalities, by creating jobs for all and by improving housing and the environment of the inner cities and council estates.

However, Young has criticized governments of all political viewpoints for failing to tackle the basic inequalities that cause the insecurity, relative deprivation, marginalization and exclusion that probably fuel most crime.

Evaluation of Left Realism

- Gordon Hughes argues that Left Realists have drawn our attention to the brutalizing and unromantic reality of inner-city street crime.
- They have also highlighted the effect of crime on victims.
- Left Realists have also shown clearly that most victims of crime are members of deprived groups – which most theories of crime have neglected.

However:

- There is little empirical evidence to support the view that young working-class or black criminals interpret their realities in the way described by Lea and Young.
- Lea and Young do not explain why the majority of working-class and African-Caribbean youth do not turn to crime.
- The theory only focuses on subcultural criminal responses and does not explain crimes such as burglary, which is committed by individuals rather than gangs.
- It also focuses exclusively on street crime and largely ignores white-collar and corporate crime.
- It fails to account for opportunist crime committed by adults.

Essential notes

It is important to understand that subcultures do not have to be deviant. Some subcultures may be based around sport or religion, and channel feelings of frustration into positive areas.

Examiners' notes

Think about how these ideas might be researched. Lea and Young are suggesting that delinquents are motivated by the way they interpret the unequal socio-economic position they are in. Therefore, unstructured interviews, which are both flexible and focused on the research subject's interpretation of reality, might be the method that would generate the most valid or true-to-life data. The sample might be composed of teenage boys, convicted of delinquency, and might qualitatively explore their perceptions of materialism, deprivation and marginalization.

Right Realist explanations of crime and deviance

Right Realists see crime, especially street crime, as a real and growing problem that undermines social cohesion and destroys social communities. They believe that people are naturally selfish, individualistic and greedy creatures. Right Realists, therefore, assume that people are 'naturally' inclined towards criminal behaviour if it can further their interests and/or if there is little chance of being caught.

Types of Right Realism

There are three main aspects to Right Realist theories of crime.

Underclass theory

Charles Murray suggests that both in the USA and the UK, a distinct lower-class subculture exists, below the working class – an **underclass** – which subscribes to deviant and criminal values rather than mainstream values and transmits this deficient culture to their children via socialization.

David Marsland argues that the welfare state is responsible for the emergence of this underclass because **welfare dependency** has undermined people's sense of commitment and obligation to support one another. People belonging to the underclass are allegedly work-shy, choosing not to work and allegedly prefer to live off state benefits.

Murray sees the underclass as generally lacking in moral values, especially commitment to marriage and family life. A large percentage of underclass children are brought up by single mothers who are allegedly often inadequate and irresponsible parents. Absent fathers mean that boys lack paternal discipline and male role models, so young males may turn to other, often delinquent, role models on the street and gain status through crime rather than supporting their families by doing a steady job. These young males are also generally hostile towards the police and authority.

As a result, Right Realists see this alleged underclass as the main cause of crime in recent years in inner-city areas and on council estates.

Key study

Simon Charlesworth used **ethnographic research** to investigate the effects of poverty and unemployment on people living on a council estate in Rotherham, South Yorkshire. He took a flat on the estate and used both participant observation and conversational interviews to document the daily lives of the poor. He found the following:

- Miserable economic conditions had a profound negative effect on people's physical and mental health.
- Many of the unemployed suffered from depression.
- Many felt robbed of identity and value because they had no job.
- Although some people were motivated by their conditions to commit crime, most did not.
- There were few signs of the anti-social underclass Murray identified.

Rational choice theory

Clarke (1980) argues that the decision to commit crime is a choice based on a rational calculation of the likely consequences. If the rewards of crime outweigh its costs, or if the rewards of crime appear to be greater than those of non-criminal behaviour, then people will be more likely to offend.

Right Realists argue that, currently, the perceived costs of crime are low, so the crime rate has increased. Criminals foresee little risk of being caught and they view punishment if they are caught as weak and ineffective.

Control theories

Travis Hirschi argues that people are generally rational in terms of their actions and choices – they weigh up the 'costs' and 'benefits' of their behaviour, and on this basis, they make choices about their actions.

Hirschi also argues that most people do not commit crimes, as they have four controls in their lives. So the cost of crime (being caught and punished) outweighs the economic and personal benefits. These controls are:

1. **Attachment** being committed to family relationships, which may be threatened by involvement in criminality
2. **Commitment** people may have invested years in education building up a career or business or home, all of which may be lost if a person is involved in crime
3. **Involvement** people may be actively involved in community life (e.g. as volunteers, magistrates, parent governors at local schools); respect and reputation would be lost if they engaged in crime
4. **Belief** people may have been brought up to be strongly committed to beliefs in rules, discipline and respect for others and the law

Hirschi suggests that these controls prevent many people from turning to crime. As people get older, they begin to acquire these controls. Younger people usually have less to lose in terms of things like attachment. For them, respect and reputation might even be enhanced by criminality.

Evaluation of Right Realism

- John Rex and Sally Tomlinson reject the idea of the underclass as a deviant subculture that is voluntarily unemployed and devoted to criminal behaviour. They point out that poverty is often caused by factors beyond the control of the poor, for example, global recession and government policies.
- There is no convincing empirical evidence that the underclass as a distinct subculture with distinctive values and behaviour exists.
- Stan Cohen argues that **New Right** thinking leads to class inequalities in victimization – the rich live in 'paranoid fortresses' or 'gated communities' guarded by technology and private security forces, thus displacing crime to poorer, less protected areas.
- **Right Realism** overstates the rationality of criminals. For example, it is doubtful whether violent crime is underpinned by rationality.

Essential notes

Like Durkheim, Hirschi is more interested in *why* most people conform. Consequently, his theory is more about social control than about criminality. However, his theory implies that young people, ethnic minorities and members of the underclass are more likely to commit crime because they are more likely to lack the four controls.

Examiners' notes

Hirschi's ideas suffer from a lack of empirical evidence to support them. Think about how questionnaires or interviews might be designed and used to investigate the validity of these ideas.

Examiners' notes

Think about a comparative approach – what two groups might be selected to take part in this research? How might we **operationalize** Hirschi's concepts of attachment, commitment, involvement and belief?

Explanations of gender differences in crime rates – feminism

Some feminist criminologists accept that women commit less crime than men. Diana Leonard believes that the major explanation for this fact is that women are more likely to conform to rules and social controls than men. However, there are signs that this commitment to the rules may be undermined by social class and age. There are six feminist explanations as to why females commit less crime than males.

1. Differential socialization

Early feminist explanations focused on differences in the socialization of males and females. Both Carol Smart and Ann Oakley suggested that males are socialized into aggressive, self-seeking and individualistic behaviour that may make them more inclined to take risks and commit criminal acts. Females, however, are socialized into a potentially less criminal set of values and norms that stress cooperation, tenderness and caring for others.

2. Differential controls

Frances Heidensohn argues that females are generally more conformist because patriarchal society imposes greater control over their behaviour. This can be illustrated in a number of ways:

- Smart notes that girls are more strictly supervised by their parents, especially outside the home. Angela McRobbie and Jenny Garber concluded that teenage girls' lives revolve around a **bedroom culture**, so they are more likely than boys to socialize with their friends in the home rather than on the streets or in other public places.
- Sue Lees notes that girls are more likely to be controlled, as many fear having a 'bad' reputation. She notes that boys in schools often use verbalized sexual labels such as 'slag' to control girls. Girls may steer clear of deviant behaviour to avoid these labels.
- Heidensohn notes that women are more likely to be controlled by their roles as wives and mothers, so have little time for illegal activity.
- Women are less likely to be in public places where crime and deviance normally occur, especially at night, because of the threat or fear of male violence or the fear of acquiring a bad reputation.

3. Rational choices

Pat Carlen notes that working-class females commit crimes because they lack the four controls that prevent most people from committing crimes (see p 27).

Carlen argues that criminal women are often women who have failed to gain qualifications and find legitimate work. They often live in poverty and are dependent on benefits. Their attachment to family life may be weak because they have been abused by family members, run away from home and/or spent time in care. Many have lived rough on the streets. Carlen argues that many of these criminal women come to the rational conclusion that crime is the only route to a decent standard of living. Having a criminal record reinforces future criminal behaviour because it makes commitment to a conventional job and family life even less likely. However, critics of this theory suggest that Carlen fails to explain why many women in poverty choose *not* to commit crime.

Examiners' notes

Feminist researchers reject survey methods such as questionnaires and structured interviews because they claim that their emphasis on **objectivity** and detachment makes them masculine methods. Oakley and Graham argue that sociologists should use methods such as unstructured interviews and observation, which allow the researcher to understand women's experiences and viewpoints. Oakley suggests that an interviewer must be prepared to invest his or her personal identity in the relationship with those being researched. This means that both parties should have a say in the content and direction of the interview. Only with this personal involvement will the people involved get to know each other, so that the interview produces highly valid data. Why might this approach be particularly useful when looking at concepts like sexual reputation?

4. The feminization of poverty

Some feminist sociologists suggest that poverty has become feminized in the last 20 years, as women have become increasingly more likely than men to experience low pay and benefits. Consequently, some types of crime dominated by females, notably shoplifting and social security fraud, may be a reaction to poverty. Sandra Walklate notes that shoplifting and prostitution are often motivated by economic necessity, for example, to provide children with food, toys and clothes.

5. Liberation theory

Freda Adler argues that as society becomes less patriarchal, so women's crime rates will rise. In other words, women's liberation from patriarchy will lead to a new type of female criminal because they will have greater opportunity and confidence to commit crime.

- Between 1981 and 1997, the number of under-18 girls convicted of violent offences in England and Wales doubled – from 65 per 100 000 to 135 per 100 000.
- A Demos survey of 2 000 UK women aged 18 to 24 found that one in eight respondents believed it was acceptable to use physical violence to get something they really wanted.

Key study

A questionnaire survey of teenage girls in Glasgow carried out by Michele Burman *et al.* found that 98.5% of girls had witnessed first-hand some form of interpersonal physical violence; 70% had witnessed first-hand five or more such incidents. Nearly two-thirds knew someone who had been physically hurt or injured by violence; 41% had experienced someone deliberately hitting, punching, or kicking them. Ten per cent of the girls described themselves as 'violent' and 10% reported having committed seven or more types of physically violent acts such as punching, kicking and hitting with an object.

Other critics point out that economic changes have benefitted mainly middle-class women. There are few signs of these women being involved in white-collar or corporate crime. Most female offenders are working class and are probably motivated by many of the same factors that motivate working-class men, for example, poverty and the feelings of humiliation, powerlessness, envy and hostility that accompany a marginalized position in society.

6. Postmodern perspectives

Hazel Croall looks at female crime from a **postmodern** perspective and suggests that teenage girls are usually motivated to commit crime by three inter-related factors:

- a drug habit (which often leads to prostitution and shoplifting)
- the excitement that often accompanies the act of committing crime
- the **conspicuous consumption** of goods such as designer label clothing, which are often the target of shoplifting.

Examiners' notes

Carlen conducted unstructured-recorded interviews with 39 working women, aged 15 to 46, who had been convicted of a range of crimes. At the times of the interviews, 20 were in custody. What problems of reliability might have occurred because of the method used? Why might the research design have produced high levels of validity in terms of the data generated by the interviews?

Examiners' notes

Self-report studies are a type of questionnaire used to investigate gender differences in committed crime. Campbell's self-report study found that the ratio of male crime to female crime is 1.5 to 1 rather than 7 to 1. However, the findings of such surveys are often undermined by over-reporting, under-reporting, ethical problems and the difficulty of finding a representative sample.

Explanations of gender differences in crime rates – masculinity

Until fairly recently, the idea that masculinity exerted a major influence on crime was generally neglected. Feminism was the first theory to draw criminological attention to the role of **gender-role socialization** in the social construction of crime. Oakley, for example, suggested that gender-role socialization in the UK, especially in working-class families, might result in boys and men subscribing to values that potentially overlap with criminality.

Oakley's ideas were developed by James Messerschmidt, who argued that boys in the UK are socialized into a **hegemonic** masculine value system that stresses differences from women, and particular masculine goals that need to be achieved in order to become a 'real man'. These goals include:

- The need to acquire respect from other men in order to maintain reputation.
- Having power, authority and control over others.
- The **objectification of women** and the celebration of masculine virility through promiscuity.
- Toughness expressed through aggression, confrontation and force.
- Territorial loyalty and honour expressed through being part of a larger group.
- Being emotionally hard and not expressing weakness by showing feelings.
- Being anti-authority, by claiming individuality and self-reliance.
- Taking risks and living life on the edge.
- Seeking pleasure, thrills and excitement to compensate for the boredom of work or unemployment.

Messerschmidt argues that working-class youth's experience of education is often one of under-achievement. Anti-social subcultures are constructed and organized around the achievement of hegemonic masculine values to compensate for the negative experience of school. These gangs operate both inside and outside of school. However, Messerschmidt notes that this need to live out masculine values is not confined to working-class youth and men. He notes that middle-class men may be motivated by this masculine value system to commit white-collar and corporate crime.

However Messerschmidt's analysis has been criticized because he fails to explain why not all men use crime to accomplish hegemonic masculine goals. The majority are law-abiding citizens. Furthermore, there is debate as to whether masculinity is a major cause of crime or whether it is merely one way in which crime is expressed. For example, is it just an expression of toughness rather than being a cause of crime?

Key study

Simon Winlow's study: The changing nature of masculinity

Winlow's study of masculinity in Sunderland suggests that most working-class men traditionally expressed their masculine values through the work they did, through their domestic roles as breadwinner and head of household and through their leisure time, which focused mainly on drinking in pubs. Opportunities to get involved in crime were fairly low and violence, when it occurred, which was fairly rare, was shaped by masculine competition for respect and status or for the attention of women.

However, the mass unemployment of the 1980s experienced in industrial communities such as Sunderland meant that men could no longer express their masculinity through their work or by being the breadwinner. Economic change often meant that women became the breadwinners. Winlow notes that young men, in particular, experienced long-term unemployment after leaving school and became dependent on benefits. Winlow argues that these young men increasingly value violence, as it offers a release from boredom and access to status. In this world, the gang becomes all-important because it provides thrills, protection, mutual support, friendship, prestige, and income to buy fashionable clothes, alcohol and drugs.

Winlow suggests that the nature of criminal opportunity has also changed because of these economic changes. Criminality is now an **entrepreneurial concern** – a means of making money. Crime and violence have become careers in themselves. For example, money can now be made:

- illegitimately, through protection rackets, dealing in drugs and/or stolen cars and loan sharking
- legitimately, by being a bouncer or security consultant.

Postmodern studies of masculinity and crime

Jackson Katz argues that young males commit crime for the pleasure or thrill that is derived from the risk of being caught or having power over others. Katz refers to these thrills as transgressions. Stephen Lyng suggests that much of crime is **edgework**, as it is located on the edge, between the thrill of getting away with it and the potential danger and uncertainty of being captured and punished. In this sense, crime is a form of gambling, providing pleasure and thrills. It allows young men who have little economic security to exercise a form of control over their lives. Katz also notes that violence, in terms of thrill and power exercised over others, is rational in the context of achieving the goals of hegemonic masculinity.

Essential notes

Winlow used a combination of unstructured interviews and covert participant observation to study masculinity in Sunderland. He trained to be a bouncer and actually became a security doorman at a nightclub where he was able to observe masculinity first-hand. What do you think were the strengths and weaknesses of this approach?

Essential notes

It is not just young males who are motivated by the excitement and danger associated with crime. Some criminologists, notably Croall, suggest female teenage crime might also be the product of this need for thrills.

Explanations of ethnic differences in crime rates

African-Caribbean people and, to a lesser extent, Asian people are over-represented in the official crime statistics (OCS) and in the prison population (see p 6).

The ethnic minority prison population has doubled in a decade – from 11 332 in 1998 to 22 421 in 2008. Over a similar period, the overall number of prisoners rose by less than two-thirds.

Most of these prisoners are male. For example, in 2007, there were 19 658 male ethnic minority prisoners constituting 26% of the total prison population. Thirty-six per cent of 15 to 18-year-old men held in youth custody in England and Wales are from black or other ethnic minority groups. Ethnic minority women are also over-represented in the criminal justice system. In 2009, 29% of the female prison population was made up of ethnic minority women.

In 2008–09, black and mixed-race people made up 17.8% of the prison population, while Asians and Chinese people constituted 8.9%. Muslims made up 12% of the prison population.

Sociological explanations of ethnic minority crime
Demographic explanations

Morris argues that according to the OCS most crime is committed by young people and that ethnic minority groups include a higher proportion of young people who have committed crimes than the white population. However, if this was the case, young Asians would also be over-represented, as the majority of Asians in the UK are under 30 years old. However, this group does not feature as heavily as young black Britons.

Interpretivist critiques of the criminal justice system

Interpretivist sociologists argue that criminal statistics do not tell us much about black or Asian criminality. They simply tell us about their involvement with the criminal justice system. The evidence suggests that the OCS may not be a true record of ethnic minority crime, but rather that the OCS may simply reflect levels of discrimination towards ethnic minorities by the police and other criminal justice agencies.

Coretta Phillips and Ben Bowling (2007) argue that since the 1970s, the black community has been subjected to oppressive military-style policing, which has resulted in the over-policing of these communities, reflected in the excessive police use of stop and search. Statistics on police stop and search, released in March 2010, reveal that police stop and search black Britons six times more than white Britons, and Asians twice as often as white Britons.

Various observational studies of police – suspect interaction suggest that the decisions of police officers to stop, search and arrest young African-Caribbean males are based on negative racial profiling or stereotyping. Simon Holdaway argues that police canteen culture is still characterized by racist language, jokes and banter and this racist culture often underpins the decision to stop black Britons. The MacPherson Report into the death of Stephen Lawrence, the black teenager, concluded that the London Metropolitan Police was guilty of 'institutional racism' in its failure to tackle such discrimination. In 2008, the Metropolitan Black Police Association actually warned people from ethnic minorities not to join the police force because of what they perceived as a hostile and racist atmosphere at many London police stations.

Key study

P. A. J. Waddington *et al.* (2004) watched CCTV footage of police officers and interviewed officers about their stop and search activities.

They found that although a disproportionate number of ethnic minority youth were stopped, this was a realistic reflection of the type of people who were on the streets at night in high crime areas.

In other words, police stop and search policies are not shaped by racial prejudice and discrimination, but by the composition of the local population.

Examiners' notes

Think about the merits of using observation to study what goes on in courtrooms. How is such observation likely to be realistically organized? Think about the strengths and weaknesses of the observational method used by Hood, and Sharp and Budd.

Research indicates the possibility of some bias in the judicial process. C. Sharp and T. Budd observed in 2005 that young black Britons have lower offence levels compared to white youth, but are more likely to be arrested, taken to court and convicted. Furthermore, compared to white Britons, black and Asian offenders are more likely to be charged rather than cautioned and remanded in custody rather than bailed. Roger Hood's (1992) study of criminal courts in the West Midlands concluded that young African-Caribbean males were more likely than young white Britons to receive custodial sentences for the same types of offences.

Self-report studies such as the Offending, Crime and Justice Survey carried out in 2003 seem to support the view that the criminal justice system may be institutionally racist because they consistently show that white Britons have a higher rate of offending than black Britons. Moreover, those offences such as violence and drug-selling, which are stereotypically associated with black youth, are more likely to be committed by white youth.

Examiners' notes

If you are required to write a general essay on the merits of interactionism or labelling theory, you can use Phillips and Bowling's findings on the policing of ethnic minorities to illustrate the labelling process.

Phillips and Bowling suggest that this negative treatment by the criminal justice system may lead some members of black communities to feel hostile towards the police. They note that young black Britons commit more street robbery than other ethnic groups and suggest that this is a product of the negative labelling that stems from constantly being stopped and searched by the police. Crime is an expression of the hostility they feel towards the police. In other words, police labelling produces a self-fulfilling prophecy, as young black Britons live up to the stereotype of potential criminals.

Key study

Ernest Cashmore, using the ideas of Merton, argues that young African-Caribbeans in Britain are encouraged like everybody else to pursue material success, but their structural opportunities are blocked by racism,

☞ This topic continues on the next two pages

failing inner-city schools and unemployment. Young black Britons experience anomie – they are aware that their situation arises from being black in a mainly white society. They turn to street crime, which Merton described as 'innovation' (see p 29) – and justify their criminal activities on the grounds that they are rejecting white society because it has failed to offer them the opportunities that white Britons take for granted.

Left Realists note that these blocked opportunities are experienced by the majority of African-Caribbeans, yet Cashmore fails to explain why only a small proportion of young black Britons actually turn to crime.

Neo-Marxist theory

Neo-Marxist, Stuart Hall, claims that the criminalization of black people began in the 1970s when the police selectively released statistics suggesting that young black Britons were most likely to be responsible for street robbery or mugging, with white Britons likely to be the victims. This initiated a moral panic, which effectively labelled young African-Caribbean population as a folk devil, or criminal threat.

According to Hall, Britain in the early 1970s was undergoing a crisis of capitalism; unemployment was high, industrial disputes were common and riots, street protests and violent demonstrations threatened the cultural dominance, or **hegemony**, of the ruling capitalist class or **bourgeoisie**.

However, the moral panic focused on mugging came to play a crucial ideological function for the capitalist ruling class in two ways:

1. It divided the working class by encouraging racist attitudes – white working-class people were encouraged by the media, the police and politicians to view the black working class as a problem. This distracted working-class members from the real cause of their problems – the mismanagement of capitalism by the ruling class.
2. It justified the introduction of more aggressive policing, particularly stop and search, and riot squads that could be used against other 'problem' groups such as strikers, protesters and demonstrators.

In Hall's view, the OCS, which show high levels of black criminality, are socially manufactured by a repressive racist state for ideological reasons.

Key study
Paul Gilroy on crime committed by young African-Caribbeans

Paul Gilroy argues that crime committed by young African-Caribbeans is political, as it is frequently motivated by their interpretation of their position in UK society. He argues that much black street crime is a conscious and deliberate reaction, and resistance to the anger of young black Britons at the way white society has historically treated black people via slavery and colonialism, and the institutional racism of life represented by police harassment and employer discrimination.

However, the fact that most young and adult African-Caribbeans are law-abiding citizens, challenges the view that crime is part of an anti-colonial or anti-racist struggle. There is also no **empirical** evidence that black youth have the political motives that Gilroy identifies. Left Realists note that most black crime is committed against other black people, rather than white people.

Left Realism

Lea and Young attempted to explain street crime committed by both working-class white and black youth. They suggest four concepts, central to understanding why some members of ethnic minorities commit crime:

	Concept	Description
1.	Relative deprivation	The poor, whose lives are undermined by social and economic factors beyond their control such as racism, feel deprived of material possessions, compared to what they see (e.g. in the media)
2.	Individualism	People are encouraged, especially by the mass media and celebrity culture, to pursue self-interest at the expense of the community
3.	Marginalization	Ethnic minorities feel frustrated and hostile, as they have little power to change the situation
4.	Subculture	People are more likely to commit crime if they find other like-minded individuals who want to aspire to material success and/or who share their anger and hostility towards society. As Pitts notes, this may mean subcultural responses such as street gangs and violence or drug-pushing

Table 8
Lea and Young's four concepts, central to understanding why some members of ethnic minorities commit crime

Tony Sewell – triple quandary theory

In Sewell's triple **quandary** theory he identifies three risk factors that are responsible for high levels of crime among African-Caribbean boys.

1. They feel that they cannot relate to mainstream culture because they believe, for example, that teachers, police officers and employers are racist and therefore working against their interests.
2. They are very influenced by the media's emphasis on conspicuous consumption – the idea that identity and status are dependent on material things such as designer labels and jewellery.
3. Many African-Caribbean boys are brought up in single-parent families. The absence of fathers means that they lack positive male role models.

Sewell argues that these three quandaries create anxiety for black boys, which is resolved by constructing subcultures or gangs. These gangs become the arena in which young black males gain respect and status from their peers by engaging in hyper-masculine activity such as violence, as well as conspicuous consumption from the proceeds of crime.

Essential notes

Sewell takes a multi-dimensional approach to black street crime. He argues that society needs to take some responsibility for racism and for exaggerating material needs through the media. However, he is also regarded as controversial because he believes that black people need to take more responsibility for their actions.

Globalization and crime

Globalization refers to the increasing interconnectedness of societies, so that what happens in one locality is shaped by distant events in another, and vice versa. It is caused by the spread of new information and media technologies, especially the internet and satellite television, cheap air travel, mass tourism, mass migration, and the increase in the number of transnational corporations that produce and market their goods and brands in a global marketplace.

Just as there is a legitimate global capitalist economy, there is also an illegitimate or criminal global economy, which Manuel Castells argues is worth over £1 trillion a year. This global criminal economy has a number of characteristics:

Global criminal networks often evolve from established local or domestic criminal networks. D. Hobbs and C. Dunningham note that crime is increasingly 'glocal' in character, meaning that it is still locally based but is now more likely to have global connections. Examples of 'glocal' trade are:

- the illegal drugs trade, worth £300–£400 billion annually. Local prices and the availability of drugs in any city in the UK depend on how efficiently global drug trade gangs can move drugs around the world while avoiding detection
- sex trafficking for prostitution
- smuggling legal goods such as alcohol, tobacco and cars
- counterfeiting designer goods and labels.

New global communications have created fresh opportunities for crime. The internet has generated new types of global fraud. These new **cyber crimes** involve:

- financial scams
- credit card fraud
- identity theft and phishing (emails sent by fraudsters claiming to be from a bank and asking for personal banking details)
- politically-motivated forms of crime, which include hacking and terrorist websites.

Many global criminal networks have developed to feed a demand from the affluent West – especially for drugs and prostitution.

Other global criminal networks have developed because of inequalities in the global capitalist economy and terms of world trade. For example, in South American countries such as Colombia and Bolivia, local farmers prefer to grow illegal crops such as the coca plant, as it brings in more money in the global economy than growing conventional crops. For example, cocaine outsells all of Colombia's other exports combined. Poverty in the developing world is also fuelling people trafficking, which involves paying criminal gangs to be smuggled to the West, where people believe they will be better off.

Essential notes

Not all criminologists agree on how to define global crime. For example, 2010 saw the emergence of the website, *Wikileaks*, which released hundreds of thousands of confidential US cables from American embassies around the world on a range of sensitive political issues. The US government views Julian Assange, who founded the site, as a criminal, whereas others see him as a crusader for democracy.

Global crime is difficult to police because international laws are ill defined and international criminal justice agencies do not have the global powers to pursue global criminals. Cooperation between international agencies is limited, or hindered by conflict between local and international police agencies and also conflict between governments.

Marxist sociologists suggest that not only global criminal gangs are responsible for global crime. Transnational corporations can also commit global crimes such as green crimes, which are damaging to the global environment. An example is illegally dumping toxic and radioactive waste in developing countries.

Furthermore, Graham Taylor notes that globalization has made it easier for elite groups and transnational corporations to move funds and profits around the world to avoid taxation. There may also be overlap between criminal organizations and the powerful wealthy elites who run the legitimate capitalist global economy, as the former invest in 'legitimate' businesses in an attempt to launder profits from crime.

Radical criminologists point out that many global crimes are committed by powerful people, who use their influence to ensure that no laws exist to criminalize their activities, and that no punishment is likely. This has led to some radical criminologists arguing that 'crime' needs to be redefined – rather than meaning 'activities that break domestic or international laws', crimes need to include all activities that harm living species and the environment in which they live. The idea of studying such harms is known as **zemiology**.

Postmodernists such as Ulrich Beck argue that global crime has created a new set of insecurities and anxieties – a global **risk consciousness**. In the past, any risk of becoming a victim of crime originated in our local environment. Increasingly, we are at risk from crime that originates thousands of miles away – global terrorism. Global risk consciousness has resulted in Western governments tightening immigration and border controls. Negatively, it has led to media hysteria about immigrants and asylum seekers and an increase in hate crimes such as racist attacks.

Taylor argues that globalization has resulted in increases in domestic crime because transnational corporations increasingly switch production away from the West to the developing world. This has led to unemployment, poverty and expanding inequalities. Moreover, the media and advertising encourage materialistic goals. The resulting strain from a lack of legitimate opportunities may encourage the poor to adopt criminal behaviour in order to achieve material goals.

Examiners' notes

Evaluation is an important skill that you must be seen to be applying while writing an essay. Think about the evaluative points you might raise about the difficulty of researching global crime. Can sociologists realistically collect **primary data** on this subject using existing research methods? What types of secondary data might be more suitable?

Examiners' notes

Evaluative thinking is important. For example, think about how difficult it is to research activities that are carried out by dangerous powerful individuals and groups in secrecy. The task is even more difficult because not all sociologists agree on what is 'criminal'.

Essential notes

Note that when it comes to explaining crime, there are considerable similarities between Marxist and functionalist approaches. This is why Marxism is sometimes described as a form of left-wing functionalism.

Green crime

Green crime refers to crime against the environment. Green crime is increasingly seen as a form of global crime for two reasons:

1. The planet is regarded as a single ecosystem in which human beings, other species and the environment are interconnected and interdependent. Harm done to other species or aspects of the environment such as the air, water supplies, the ocean and the rainforest are increasingly seen as impacting negatively on the quality and future of human life wherever it is in the world. For example, radioactive fallout from the Chernobyl nuclear reactor disaster of 1986 spread thousands of miles across Europe, resulting in the banning of sheep farming in parts of England and Wales.

2. Green crime generally tends to be carried out by powerful interests, particularly transnational corporations such as oil and chemical companies working with the cooperation of nation states and local wealthy elites.

Manufactured risks

Ulrich Beck points out that many of the threats to the ecosystem are **manufactured risks** and are the result of the massive demand for consumer goods and the technology that underpins it. Human demand for manufactured goods has potentially negative effects for both humanity and the environment, in that increasing greenhouse gas emissions are contributing to global warming and climate change, and the possibility of future disasters such as flooding. Beck notes that we now live in societies threatened by global risks.

Policing green crime

However, green crime is extremely difficult to police for two main reasons:

1. There are very few local or international laws governing the state of the environment. International laws are particularly difficult to construct because not all countries agree to sign up to global agreements. For example, both China and the USA have been reluctant to agree to meet international targets to reduce carbon emissions.

2. Many of the laws that do exist are shaped by powerful capitalist interests, especially global 'big business'. Governments, especially in the developing world, are generally reluctant to rein in transnational corporations because they are dependent on the income these companies generate. Enforcement of laws that do exist to protect the environment is often weak.

Radical criminologists such as Rob White argue that the present criminal law is inadequate for dealing with green crime. He takes a more radical approach and argues that green crime should be defined as 'any action that harms the physical environment and any of the creatures that live within it, even if no law has been technically broken'. White points out that many of the worst environmental harms committed by big business or the state are not actually illegal and therefore not criminal. Moreover, he

Examiners' notes

Note that Beck's observations are also relevant to sociology as a science debate (see p 68). Postmodernists argue that, increasingly, people are becoming disillusioned with science because it has negative by-products, which may eventually threaten human existence.

Examiners' notes

Think about your evaluative approach to this zemiological eco-centric view of green crime. There are problems of interpretation – what counts as 'harm'? and ideology – who defines what counts as crime?

argues that current laws are inconsistent in that they often differ across different countries, and are biased in that they are often too influenced by businesses with a vested interest in doing harm to the environment because their business is the extraction of raw materials or the exploitation of natural environments such as rainforests. White argues that only a green criminology that is focused on the idea of environmental harm can develop a truly global perspective on green crimes.

White argues that green criminology takes an **eco-centric** view of environmental harm – it sees such harm as damage to the environment and/or other species of creature, and ultimately to the future of the human race. This view opposes the more **anthropocentric** view of big business, which assumes that humans have the right to exploit the environment and other species for their own benefit. White argues that this capitalist ideology is responsible for a great deal of environmental harm.

Key study

Nigel South classifies green crime into primary crimes and secondary crimes.

Primary crimes are the direct result of the destruction and degradation of the planet's resources and include:

- crimes of air pollution such as industrial carbon and greenhouse gas emissions
- crimes of **deforestation** such as illegal logging
- crimes of species decline and animal rights
- crimes of fresh water and marine pollution such as oil spillages.

South identifies secondary green crimes as those which involve flouting existing laws and regulations, for example:

- dumping toxic waste, particularly in the developing world
- breaches of health and safety rules, causing disasters such as Chernobyl and Bhopal
- offloading products such as pharmaceuticals onto Third World markets after they have been banned on safety grounds in the West.

Some governments have taken very aggressive and often illegal steps to deal with environmental movements such as Greenpeace, which have been very vocal in identifying green crime and its perpetrators.

Evaluation of green criminology

- Green criminology recognizes the growing importance of environmental issues and manufactured global risks.
- It recognizes the interdependence of humans, other species and the environment.
- However, its focus on harm rather than criminality means that green criminology is often accused of being engaged with subjective interpretation rather than objective scientific analysis, and is therefore biased.

Essential notes

Operationalizing means the measurement of abstract concepts by defining them in research such as by writing questionnaire questions. For example, crime is easy to measure because it is defined legally but harm is more difficult to define and measure because it is often a matter of interpretation.

Examiners' notes

It would make sense to use green crime to illustrate the **criminogenic** nature of capitalism if an exam essay title focuses on Marxist explanations of crime and deviance.

Human rights and state crime

State crime is defined as those illegal activities carried out by the agents of the state such as the armed services, the secret services, civil servants, the police and prison services on behalf of governments and political leaders in order to further state interests. Such activities are illegal in that they break domestic or international laws.

Most criminologists accept that crimes committed by states across the world would probably include **genocide**, **ethnic cleansing**, the use of torture, assassination of political opponents, supporting terrorist activities against elected governments and invading less powerful states.

Some criminologists have focused on how the state represses its own citizens and have looked at the number of questionable deaths in police custody and suicides in prison, as well as shootings by the police.

Eugene McLaughlin has also identified censorship of the media and institutional racism as state crimes. Herman Schwendinger argues that definitions of state crimes should be extended to include human rights crimes. He suggests that any violation of people's human rights should be defined as illegal and therefore criminal. However, Schwendinger's definition of human rights is broad. He suggests that if some groups are denied the same opportunities as the majority population on the basis of racism, sexism and **homophobia**, or if they are economically exploited, then, the unequal conditions that result are the result of crimes against human rights.

Disagreement about state crime

There is much disagreement about what constitutes state crime for the following reasons:

- State crime is carried out by powerful people or groups who can define their activities as being legitimate. This makes measuring the extent of state crimes difficult, especially as these activities are often carried out by the most secretive agencies of the state. Governments have the power and resources to cover up such activities and can actually control the flow of information and especially the media by issuing legal instructions to prevent journalists from speaking about state crimes, in the 'public interest'.
- The powerful can impose their definition as to what counts as crime on society. What is defined as crime or violence is an ideological construct. Governments have the power to define killing as a problem if it is done by a member of the public, but as justified if done by a police officer or soldier. This ideological relativity can be seen with regard to who the powerful define as terrorists or freedom fighters, and what counts as a 'war crime'. For example, the Holocaust has been defined as a war crime, but dropping the atom bomb on the Japanese cities Hiroshima and Nagasaki was defined by the West as 'necessary'.

- Stan Cohen criticizes Schwendinger's view that state crime should include violations of human rights. Cohen notes that genocide and torture are clearly crimes, but argues that economic exploitation is not clearly criminal, even if it is morally unacceptable. Furthermore, he argues there is not enough agreement as to what constitutes human rights. For example, most people accept that freedom should be a human right but not everyone would agree that freedom from poverty is a right.

- Cohen argues that it is difficult to find out the true extent of state crime because governments either deny their actions or attempt to justify their actions in an attempt to cover up their illegal nature. For example, if denial of a massacre does not work, the state will suggest that it was **collateral damage** or that it was necessary to protect national security.

- Cohen notes that perpetrators of crimes on behalf of the state do not see themselves as criminal. He argues that they use **techniques of neutralization** to deny or justify crimes against people. For example, they deny their victims by labelling them terrorists or extremists. They deny the injury or damage by suggesting that the other side started it, and they deny responsibility by saying they were simply obeying orders or doing their duty. These perpetrators often appeal to a higher cause – for example, the defence of the free world – to legitimize their actions and appear less criminal.

- Herbert Kelman and V. Lee Hamilton also note that many state crimes are 'crimes of obedience' – people commit them because they have been socialized into believing it is their duty to obey and that their behaviour is acceptable and necessary (rather than criminal) because the enemy are animals and monsters to which the normal rules of morality do not apply.

- Critics of the concept of 'state crime' argue that the so-called 'criminality' of the act may be outweighed by the fact that the act was committed in the national interest. Some argue that it may be necessary to go beyond the limits of the law in defeating terrorism, so that assassination and torture are 'necessary evils'.

Essential notes

Cohen suggests that Schwendinger is confusing immorality with criminality. Schwendinger is clearly taking a highly moral value position and is attempting to impose that position on the world of criminology. This is highly relevant to the theory and method debate about whether sociologists should be neutral scientists in search of objective truth or people who aim to change the world 'for the better'. Schwendinger is clearly in the latter camp.

Examiners' notes

This is a new area of criminology and therefore is still evolving. However, it is important to be evaluative in order to maximize your marks. For example, you may have noticed that the study of state crime is over-reliant on particular types of secondary data, especially public and historical documents, expressive documents such as diaries and mass media reports. Be aware of the strengths and weaknesses of these research strategies.

The mass media and crime

Moral panics

Moral panic theory originates in interactionist theory. A moral panic refers to intense public concern or anxiety about a social problem or social group that has been brought to public attention by the mass media, especially the tabloid newspapers. The moral panic usually amplifies the threat of the problem or group out of all proportion to its real seriousness.

Key study

Stan Cohen: Folk devils and moral panics

The terms 'folk devil' and 'moral panic' were first used by Stan Cohen in his analysis of the social reaction to various incidents involving mods and rockers at UK coastal resorts in 1964.

Moral panics usually go through the following stages:

- The media report a particular event or group in a negative and stereotypical way, using sensationalist, emotional and exaggerated headlines and language.
- Follow-up articles engage in the **demonization** of the group and consequently construct the group as folk devils.
- The media engage in **symbolization** – focusing on the symbols of the group in terms of dress, hairstyles and music, which it associates with trouble and violence, so that the group becomes visible to the general public.
- The media invites people with influence – **moral entrepreneurs** such as politicians, experts and bishops – to condemn the group or behaviour.
- The media predicts further trouble from the group.
- This puts pressure on the authorities – politicians, police and courts – to curb the problem group and activity and therefore control it. Increased policing and severe judicial punishments often result at this stage.
- A self-fulfilling prophecy develops as the group resists the attempts to control it or acts up to the media, which leads to arrests and a spiral of further negative reporting.

Moral panic theorists such as Cohen, and Jock Young, note that moral panics often result in deviancy amplification – the media reaction worsens the problem they initially set out to condemn. What was initially a fantasy problem becomes a very real problem.

Why moral panics occur

There are various explanations about why moral panics occur:

- Moral panics seem to arise most often when society is undergoing a 'moral crisis'. Such crises are usually linked to major social change or modernization; for example, the first moral panics about youth in the 1950s and 1960s coincided with youth becoming a consumer group in its own right, with its own very distinctive values and norms, which were often viewed as immoral and threatening by the older generation. Cohen suggested that the emergence of youth cultures was seen by the older generation as undermining both the moral order and traditional authority.

- Marxists such as Stuart Hall have argued that moral panics are used by the capitalist state to divert attention from the mismanagement of capitalism and especially wealth and income inequalities. Hall claims that in the 1970s, British capitalism experienced a 'crisis of hegemony', meaning that the cultural domination of the ruling class, and especially their right to govern, was challenged by economic recession, rapidly rising inflation, unemployment and industrial action. However, Hall claims that a moral panic focused on the persistent media reporting of a crime such as a mugging or street robbery, allegedly carried out by young black people, served the ideological purpose of turning the white working class against the black working class. This classic 'divide and rule' strategy diverted attention from the mismanagement of capitalism.
- However, in criticism of Marxism, it is very difficult to uncover evidence of collusion between the ruling class, the police and the media to purposely create moral panics that act as political diversions.

Examiners' notes

Questions on moral panics can appear in their own right so it is important that you have a developed knowledge of this social phenomena. However, if a more general question on the relationship between crime and media should appear, you will need to balance moral panics alongside other aspects of media coverage of crime and the idea that the mass media might be partially responsible for increases in particular types of crime.

Key study

Jack Fawbert on 'hoodies'

Jack Fawbert analysed the media coverage of 'hoodies', particularly the banning of hoodies at the Bluewater Shopping Centre in 2005. Fawbert concludes that the media coverage fulfilled all the criteria of a moral panic.

- Some commentators claim that moral panics do not reflect social or moral anxieties held by the majority of society's members – rather that they are quite simply the product of the desire of journalists and editors to sell newspapers. They are a good example of how audiences are manipulated by the media for commercial purposes.
- Left Realists argue that moral panics are often based on reality or fact – the groups identified are often a very real threat to those living in inner-city areas. Left Realists, however, note that moral panic theorists often deny the reality of the subject matter of moral panics and portray them as fantasies made up by journalists. Young and John Lea note that portraying such crime as a fantasy product of the mass media is naïve because such crime has real negative outcomes for people living in inner-city areas.

John Muncie notes that, like labelling theory, moral panic theory has drawn our attention to the role and power of the media in defining normal and deviant behaviour. It has given us some sociological insight into the consequences of labelling in terms of how labelled groups react to media demonization. The moral panic thesis also reminds us to continually question our commonsensical understanding of crime and especially the media reporting of crime.

Angela McRobbie and Sarah Thornton argue that the concept of moral panic is now outdated in this era of sophisticated media technology and 24-hour rolling news. Most events are no longer reported for long enough to sustain the interest that traditional moral panics generated in the past.

Media representations of crime

News does not just happen – it is a socially manufactured product. This means that it is the end result of a complex process involving journalists and editors applying a set of criteria known as **news values** to judge if a story is newsworthy, or whether it will attract an audience.

Crime is newsworthy because bad news, rather than good news, attracts audiences. Violent and sexual crimes are generally viewed as more newsworthy than property crime, as these crimes are more easily personalized and usually more dramatic. Crimes such as murder, kidnap and stranger rape are newsworthy because they are relatively rare. Crime is often reported as a human interest story, in the sense that it could happen to anyone.

However, such news values can result in crime reporting not representing the true reality of crime. Jason Ditton and James Duffy found that 46% of media reports were about violent or sexual crimes, although these types of crimes only made up 3% of crimes recorded by the police. There is also evidence of increasing preoccupation with sex crimes. Keith Soothill and Sylvia Walby (1991) found that newspaper reporting of rape cases increased from under one-quarter of all cases in 1951 to over one-third in 1985.

Key study

Richard Felson argues that media reporting reinforces certain fallacies or falsehoods about crime:

Age fallacy – media representations give the impression that all age groups are involved in crime

Class fallacy – the media give the impression that the middle class are more likely to be victims of crime, yet the poor are most likely to be victims

Ingenuity fallacy – the media give the impression that criminals are clever, yet most crime is in fact opportunistic; it is done on the spur of the moment

Police fallacy – the media may give the impression that the police are more efficient than they really are

Dramatic fallacy – the media focus only on the most violent crimes, thus creating fear of crime; media reporting may encourage fear of crime, especially among the elderly and women, by over-focusing on crimes against these groups.

The media as a possible cause of crime

There has long been concern that media content has a negative effect on the behaviour of young people, especially children. Television, films, comics, music lyrics (especially rap), the internet and computer games have all been accused of causing violence and anti-social behaviour.

It is suggested that some audiences may imitate violent, immoral or anti-social behaviour seen on television or in the cinema. The media is regarded as a powerful secondary agent of socialization, which shapes the behaviour of young people and produces a copycat effect.

It is also suggested that media content has encouraged crime and deviance by exposing vulnerable groups such as children to deviant role-models and **desensitizing** them to the effects of violence through repeated viewings. The media has also been accused of transmitting knowledge of criminal techniques, portraying the police as incompetent and glamourizing crime.

Literally thousands of studies into the link between the media and crime have been conducted. However, most sociologists note that this link is simplistic because it fails to recognize that audiences differ in terms of factors such as age, social class, intelligence and level of education and consequently do not react in the same way to media content. The argument also fails to appreciate the nature of violence – most experts argue that it is caused by a complex range of factors: poor socialization, bad parenting, peer group influences, mental illness, drugs or alcohol.

Key study

David Morrison showed a range of violent film clips to groups of women, young men and war veterans. All the groups thought that a very violent scene from the film *Pulp Fiction* was humorous because there was light-hearted dialogue.

However, a scene from *Ladybird, Ladybird*, showing domestic violence, caused distress for all three groups because of the realism of the setting, the perceived unfairness and because child actors were part of the scene. Morrison concludes that the context in which violence on screen takes place affects its impact on the audience.

Richard Sparks notes that many media effects studies ignore the meanings that viewers give to media violence. There is evidence that audiences interpret violence in cartoons, horror films and news quite differently. For example, David Buckingham's research into how children use the media suggests that even very young children are **media literate** and use the media in a responsible way.

Guy Cumberbatch reviewed over 3 500 studies on the relationship between the media and violence and failed to find one that proved the connection. None disproved it either. As he concludes, 'the jury is still out on this issue'.

Some **neo-functionalist** and Marxist sociologists suggest the media is responsible for crime by stimulating the desire for money or unaffordable consumer goods through advertising. Robert Reiner argues that the mass media help to increase people's sense of relative deprivation and the outcome of this may be that some people turn to crime.

Examiners' notes

It is crucial that any reference to this debate is sociologically sophisticated and not over-reliant on expressing commonsense assumptions as 'facts'. Many people automatically believe there is a connection between violent films and real-life murder because of the publicity given to this by tabloid newspapers and politicians. The sociological debate is much more complex and your account should reflect this.

Essential notes

Many sociological theories believe that the media have some sort of impact on society. Marxists and neo-functionalists believe that advertising and stories about celebrities fuel alienation and anomie, respectively. Marxists also believe that mass media content is shaped by ruling class ideology in order to disguise the true extent of class inequality. Feminists too see a connection between sexual crime and pornography. However, with the research methods that are available to sociologists, these theories are difficult to prove in terms of collecting sociological evidence.

Victimization

The British Crime Survey

Victim (or victimization) surveys are an attempt to gain a better understanding of the reality of crime than is provided by the official crime statistics (OCS). The British Crime Survey (BCS), conducted by the Home Office, is a major victim survey that was started in 1983. It is now conducted annually.

The BCS is a face-to-face survey. Originally, during 1983 and 2006, it targeted between 8 000 and 11 000 people. However, the 2008 survey conducted 46 983 face-to-face structured interviews with a sample of people aged 16 and over living in private households in England and Wales. Twenty-two trained interviewers used laptop computers to record the responses. Using **random sampling** (to give every member of the sample an equal chance of being selected), rather than **non-random-sampling** (whereby every member of the sample population would not have an equal chance of being in the sample), a sample is selected from the Postcode Address File. The BCS sample is designed to be as nationally representative as possible in order to **generalize** the results to the country as a whole. The overall **response rate** in 2007 was 76%, although this is lower in inner-city areas.

The **interview schedule**, or questionnaire, is composed of pre-coded **closed questions** with fixed choice responses to make it easy to quantify and turn into statistical data. The interview schedule takes about 48 minutes to complete, and has questions about personal experiences of being a crime victim during the past year. The focus is on property crimes such as vehicle-related thefts and burglary, and violent crimes such as assaults.

The findings of the BCS

Over the years, data collected from the BCS have suggested that:

- Throughout the 1990s, a minority of crimes (one in four) were reported to the police – this suggested that police-recorded crime statistics were the tip of a much larger crime iceberg. However, the latest BCS statistics indicate that the gap between crime reported to the BCS and crimes reported to and recorded by the police is at its most narrow since 1983. This confirms that crime is now falling.
- BCS data confirms that the majority of crimes in 2009 are still property related.
- Violent crime represents around a fifth (21%) of BCS crime, compared to the 19% shown in police statistics. However, half of violent crime involves no injury and since 2007, BCS violent crime has fallen by 12%.
- The risk of becoming a victim of crime has fallen from 24% to 22%, representing nearly one million fewer victims. Overall, only 3% of adults faced violent crime in the last year.
- BCS data suggests that women worry more about all crimes, except vehicle crime. However, the surveys also show that people who fear

violent crime most (the elderly and women) are least likely to be victims. Conversely, people who fear crime least (young men) are most likely to be victims.

The strengths of the BCS

The BCS is thought to provide a reliable reflection of the actual extent of household and personal crime because it includes crimes not reported to or recorded by the police. Supporters of the BCS claim that these surveys are more valid than the OCS, as they uncover the dark figure of crime – crimes not reported to the police and therefore not recorded. The BCS is also unaffected by changes in police counting rules.

The use of structured interviews offers greater opportunity for reliable data because both questions and responses are standardized and the interviews are piloted in advance.

The limitations of BCS methodology

However, the survey does have some weaknesses:

- It does not cover commercial victimization such as thefts from businesses and shops, and fraud.
- It excludes victimless crimes such as possession of drugs and prostitution.
- It does not currently cover crimes against children, although it will in future years.
- Ellington argues that the samples used by the BCS are not representative of the national population because owner-occupiers and 16- to 24-year-olds are generally over-represented, whereas the unemployed are under-represented.
- The BCS is not really 'British', as it does not cover Scotland and Northern Ireland.
- The BCS relies on victims having objective knowledge of the crimes committed against them but people's memories of traumatic events are often unreliable.
- People may be unaware that they have been victims – especially children or the elderly.
- Marxists point out that the general public are usually unaware that they may have been victims of crimes committed by the economically powerful such as corporate crimes.
- Pilkington notes that the BCS distorts the meaning of the numbers – violent and sexual offences against the person may constitute a relatively small proportion of recorded offences, but these crimes often have a more traumatic effect on victims, compared to property crime.
- Left and Right Realist sociologists argue that the BCS tells us little about the day-to-day experience of living in high crime areas such as the inner city or problem council estates.

Examiners' notes

The BCS is a good example of criminology in practice, so questions are likely to appear in the Methods in Context section of the exam paper. Remember, your response to essay questions should be evaluatively balanced – focus on strengths and weaknesses.

Essential notes

Interpretivist researchers are generally critical of methods such as structured interviews, as they are inflexible and rarely allow researchers access to **qualitative data** about people's motives, feelings and fears. The use of pre-coded answers restricts respondents' choices of response to the sociologist's interpretation of the reality. Interpretivists argue that structured interviews are artificial devices that create barriers between researchers and their samples.

☞ **This topic continues on the next two pages**

Essential notes

Interpretivist sociologists argue that unstructured interviews can produce more validity in terms of the quality of data because they place the interviewee at the centre of the research. Unstructured interviews are not restricted by pre-planned questions and tick boxes. A skilled interviewer is flexible and will allow the interviewee free rein for discussion. Skilful probing usually uncovers motives and interpretations so that the researcher is able to get 'inside the head' of those being researched and to see the social world through their eyes.

Essential notes

Most feminist research into aspects of the family, what goes on in schools and classrooms, health care and female victimization has used interpretivist methodology, particularly unstructured interviews and participant observation. Feminists believe that questionnaires and structured interviews involve researchers imposing their power and interpretations on research subjects in much the same way that men impose their version of social reality on women in patriarchal societies.

Realist victim surveys

An alternative approach to the BCS has been developed by Realist sociologists, who suggest that the BCS has tended to neglect the concentration of crime in the inner city and deprived council estates.

The Islington Crime Survey (ICS) was carried out by Left Realist sociologists, John Lea and Jock Young, using sympathetic unstructured interviewing techniques. They asked victims living in inner London about serious crime such as sexual assault, domestic violence and racial attacks and found that a full third of all households had been touched by serious crime in the previous 12 months.

The ICS found that crime shaped people's lives to a considerable degree – a quarter of all people always avoided going out after dark because of fear of crime and 28% felt unsafe in their own homes. Women experienced a curfew on their activities – over half the women never went out after dark because of their fear of crime. Lucia Zedner noted that this fear was both realistic in the context of this urban area and rational when the extent of unreported rape is taken into account.

Other Realist surveys found that fear of crime is highest among the poor, which reflects the fact that they are most at risk from crime. The Merseyside Crime Survey, for example, carried out by R. Kinsey in 1984, found that in terms of quantity and impact of crime, the poor suffer more than the wealthy from the effects of crime.

Feminist victim surveys

Feminist victim surveys tend to produce qualitative data on female victims of male crimes, most notably domestic violence and sexual attacks in which the main perpetrators are male.

Feminists are critical of the structured interview method used by the BCS. They note that in structured interviews the researcher takes an active role when asking questions. However, the interviewee takes a passive role as a mere object of study, with no role in deciding the subject or direction of the interview. Feminists argue that this mirrors the gender divisions and hierarchies of patriarchal society.

Hilary Graham (1983) claims that questionnaires and structured interviews give a distorted and invalid picture of women's experience. They impose the researcher's categories on women and make it difficult for them to express their experiences. Graham argues that sociologists should use methods that allow the researcher to understand women's experiences and viewpoints such as unstructured interviews or observation. A number of feminist victim surveys have therefore aimed to give voice to women's experiences of crime.

Key study

Dobash and Dobash: First victim survey on domestic violence

The first victim survey on domestic violence was conducted by the husband and wife team, Rebecca and Russell Dobash, in Scotland in 1980. Their two female researchers conducted 109 unstructured interviews with women who had experience of such violence – 42 of the women were living or had been living in a women's refuge.

Dobash and Dobash found that 23% of the sample had experienced violence before their marriage but believed it would cease once they were married. The other 77% had not experienced violence, and when they identified anger in men, they saw it as an indicator of how serious the man was about them, rather than as a sign of the violence to come. The first violent episode usually consisted of a single blow with little physical injury. It was often preceded by an argument, usually about the husband's possessiveness and his ideas about his wife's responsibility to him. This was usually followed by shock, shame and guilt from both parties. The husband begged for forgiveness and promised it would not happen again, while the wife tried to understand the action in terms of her own behaviour – that perhaps she had brought it upon herself. Few women responded with physical force.

Dobash and Dobash found that such violence became 'routine' and 'normal'. They found that men felt they had the right to punish or 'discipline' their wives for being 'bad' wives or mothers. Women, too, expected domestic violence to be a 'normal' part of their marriage, and consequently rarely complained about it or sought medical attention.

- Sandra Walklate's victim surveys, based on unstructured interviews, found that many female victims of domestic violence are unable to leave their partners because of the gendered power relationships that shape and govern women's lives:
  - They are less likely to have economic resources for potential independence.
  - They have nowhere else to go (the number of women's refuges in the UK is in decline).
  - They often blame themselves.
  - Threats of further violence and losing their children undermine their confidence.
- Linda Kelly's research into 'survivors' of domestic violence found that many women were undermined by verbal abuse as well as physical violence.
- Feminist researchers, Jalna Hanmer and Sheila Saunders, conducted a series of unstructured interviews with women living in one randomly selected street in Leeds during the 1980s using sympathetic and well-trained female interviewers. They found that 20% of these women had been sexually assaulted but had not reported the crime.

Examiners' notes

The debate about victim surveys is essentially a debate about methodology. The BCS is focused on achieving quantitative data, whereas Realist and feminist surveys aim to achieve empathetic understanding, or *verstehen*, and consequently qualitative data.

Control and prevention of crime

Strategies for the prevention and control of crime have generally come from two broad sociological sources – Right Realism and Left Realism (see pp 24–27). Both theories are concerned with explaining and preventing those crimes that negatively impact upon the daily lives of ordinary people. However, their focus is often quite different, as described below.

Right Realists	Emphasize the individual. They note that people choose to commit crime because the benefits outweigh the costs. So society needs to look at ways to increase the costs of crime.
Left Realists	Focus on the organization of society, and especially the inequality, disadvantage and poverty that result from this and which create the environment in which crime might be the norm.

Table 9
The focus of Right Realists and of Left Realists

Situational crime prevention

Situational crime prevention (SCP) refers to Right Realist measures aimed at reducing opportunities for crime. It focuses on encouraging potential victims to 'design out' crime by making themselves 'harder targets' by investing in more security and surveillance. The aim is to increase the risk of the criminal being caught and/or deterring criminality by reducing the opportunity for crime.

There is some evidence that car manufacturers' investment in satellite technology, disabling devices and computerized locking systems has reduced the level of car theft in the UK. It is also argued that increased surveillance in shops via CCTV, or security guards and store detectives, increases the likelihood of shoplifters being caught.

Evaluation of situational crime prevention

- Marcus Felson and Ronald V. Clarke argue that SCP strategies displace, rather than reduce crime. Criminals simply move to where targets are softer. For example, Jan M. Chaiken *et al.* found that a crackdown on subway robberies in New York merely displaced them to the streets above.
- Marxists note that SCP often creates a new type of social inequality – the poor are disproportionately the main victims of crime because the middle class can afford to invest in making themselves harder targets and therefore design crime out of their lives.
- Marxists note that SCP ignores white-collar, corporate and state crimes, which are more costly to society.
- Some sociologists have questioned the Right Realist stress on the rational nature of street crime and have suggested instead that most violent crimes are caused either by the need to feed a drug habit or by too much alcohol.
- Marxists and Left Realists argue that SCP ignores the root causes of crime such as poverty and inequality.
- The use of surveillance may be a problem because camera operators may subscribe to similar stereotypes to police officers and

Examiners' notes

All solutions to crime adopted by governments are social policies. Therefore the material on situational, environmental and Left Realist crime prevention solutions is useful to illustrate any Theory and Method question on the relationship between social policy and sociology.

consequently focus excessively on young males. This labelling may mean that the behaviour of particular groups is more likely to gain the attention of the police and courts.

Environmental crime prevention

Environmental crime prevention (ECP) is an approach that is influenced a great deal by Right Realist, James Q. Wilson. He argues that crime is caused by 'incivilities' or anti-social behaviour such as vandalism, graffiti, drugs being openly pushed and used in public places, dog fouling, littering, swearing out loud and physical harassment of groups such as the elderly. If these behaviours are tolerated and allowed to continue, areas deteriorate, as a sense of 'anything goes' develops. Wilson uses the example of broken windows. If signs of disorder such as a few broken windows are left unrepaired or graffiti is not removed, this encourages further similar deviance. Failure to deal with these problems sends out a clear signal to criminals and deviants that no one cares, encouraging more of the same.

Wilson notes that such disorder is likely to occur if there is little sense of community or neighbourhood, as this means that both formal and informal social controls are usually weak. Members of the community may feel powerless and older members may be afraid to leave their homes. Respectable people may move away and more anti-social elements may replace them. The police may feel that anti-social behaviour is not their responsibility, as they target more serious types of crime.

Wilson notes that public housing estates are more likely to experience social problems such as drugs, graffiti and vandalism and these are more likely to be found around high-rise tower blocks. Wilson argues that these problems arise because residents do not take responsibility for the common entrances, stairwells and lifts. As a result, anti-social elements take over.

Wilson proposes a number of environmental solutions:

- Any sign of environmental decline such as broken windows or graffiti must be tackled immediately, otherwise neighbourhood deterioration will follow.
- All public housing buildings should not exceed three floors and all residents should be encouraged to take responsibility for communal space, so as to protect it from outsiders.
- The police should aggressively tackle all types of crime and disorder and not just react to serious crime. This type of **zero tolerance** was famously adopted in New York to tackle, for example, subway graffiti, fare dodging, drug dealing and begging. Between 1993 and 1996, all types of crime declined dramatically, although critics suggest this had more to do with a decline in the availability of crack cocaine than with zero tolerance policing.

Essential notes

Note that this approach is very similar to and has been influenced by the ecological theory of Clifford R. Shaw and Henry D. McKay. The concept of 'tipping' (see p 17) is relevant here.

Examiners' notes

Any essay question on crime in urban areas, or cities, can refer to Wilson's theory and solutions.

Examiners' notes

Any essay on Realism should include a detailed discussion and evaluation of Realist solutions to crime.

☞ **This topic continues on the next two pages**

Left Realist solutions to crime should be cited in any essay which asks why the poor or ethnic minorities seem to commit more crime than other sections of society. This material is also essential in answering questions on urban crime.

Social and community crime prevention

Left Realists and other critical criminologists such as Marxists argue that both SCP and ECP are doomed to failure because they are treating the symptoms rather than the cause of the social disease of crime. They argue that politicians need to address the economic and social conditions – poverty, unemployment, poor housing, poor education, low pay and racial discrimination – that bring about the risk conditions for crime, particularly among the young and some ethnic minority groups. Left Realists argue that urban crime is a rational response to a lack of legitimate opportunities and the powerlessness that deprived groups feel in terms of improving their situation.

Left Realists argue that economic and social reform programmes need to be administered by governments if crime is to be seriously reduced in inner-city areas and on sink council estates.

These policies should include:

- educational programmes aimed at improving educational success in inner-city comprehensives and reducing both exclusion and the number of 16-year-olds leaving school with no qualifications
- minimum pay legislation to ensure that people are paid a fair wage so that they are not tempted to become welfare-dependent
- a reduction in wealth and income inequalities, perhaps through taxation
- economic investment in poorer urban communities to create jobs.

Generally, Left Realists argue that there should be a more coordinated attempt to improve people's economic and social opportunities. If people truly feel that the UK is meritocratic, they may be less likely to experience relative deprivation and powerlessness, and therefore the humiliation of poverty and the resulting resentment that fuels most crime.

However, these ideas have been criticized as being soft on crime and criminals because they imply that crime is society's fault, rather than the individual's choice. Furthermore, Left Realists fail to explain why most people living in poverty do not commit crime. Right Realists argue that Left Realists make excuses for criminals, and that tighter controls, more effective socialization of children and more severe punishment are the main means by which society should reduce crime.

Punishment

One measure that most people believe is effective in preventing and reducing crime is punishment, especially prison, which they believe can reduce crime in a number of ways:

	Way in which it reduces crime
Deterrence	The Right Realist position suggests that 'prison works', as prison deters many potential offenders away from crime; that is, it increases the costs of crime
Incapacitation	Right Realists argue that prison is important because it removes known criminals from the street so they cannot offend again. (Note: in some other societies, incapacitation can involve cutting off people's hands, chemical castration and capital punishment; in California, it has involved the 'three strikes and you're out' policy – committing even a minor third offence can lead to a lengthy prison sentence)
Rehabilitation	Some people believe that punishment can be used to reform or change offenders so that they will not return to their criminal careers; education and training in vocational skills are encouraged so that prisoners can earn an honest living once released

Table 10
Ways in which it is believed that prison can reduce crime

Does prison work?

The UK has invested heavily in prisons and, as a result, the prison population rose from about 60 000 in 1997 to 77 000 in 2006 and 83 000 in 2007. It was projected to rise to 90 000 by 2010 on current rates. The UK has more life-sentenced prisoners than the whole of the rest of Western Europe combined. However, there is fierce debate about whether this policy is working or not.

Roger Matthews (1997) argues that the scale of imprisonment has little effect on the crime rate. He argues that rather than reducing crime, prisons act as 'universities of crime' and that they are an 'expensive way of making bad people worse'. At best, prisons are simply 'warehouses' in which the reasons for offending are very rarely addressed and little attempt is made to reform or rehabilitate the offender. Matthews also points out that a substantial section of the prison population should not be in prison because they are either drug addicts or they are mentally ill. These people need treatment rather than punishment.

E. Solomon (2006) suggests that many people are being imprisoned for relatively minor offences for which community punishments may be more suitable. Many people whose offences would not have attracted a custodial sentence in the past are now being sent to prison. Matthews suggests that up to 50% of the prison population have committed minor offences for which prison is inappropriate and possibly damaging.

Finally, the high rates of **recidivism** (repeat offending) suggest that prison does not deter. Two-thirds of released prisoners re-offend, as do 71% of juvenile offenders, within two years of release. The overall evidence suggests that prison is not radically changing the behaviour of repeat offenders.

Examiners' notes

Questions on social control usually focus on why most people conform to the rules and do not commit crime. A discussion of the merits of punishment such as prison, as well as Émile Durkheim's emphasis on socialization into **value consensus** (see p 12) and Travis Hirschi's cost-benefit analysis (see p 27), would be appropriate to answering a question on this topic.

The sociological study of suicide

Émile Durkheim and suicide

Émile Durkheim produced the classic sociological study *Le Suicide* in 1897, which illustrates two key ideas.

1. Durkheim was a positivist sociologist, who believed that even a supremely 'individual' act such as suicide was influenced by society.
2. He believed that sociology was a science. His study of suicide was intended as an illustration of scientific enquiry in sociology.

As his main source of data, Durkheim used 19th century official statistics of suicide taken from a range of European societies for the period 1840–70. He noted three trends:

1. Within single societies the suicide rate remains constant over time.
2. The suicide rate varies constantly between different societies.
3. The suicide rate varies constantly between different groups within the same society.

Durkheim argued that constancy of suicide rates across Europe meant that they were **social facts**, determined by the nature or structure of societies.

Durkheim used the **comparative method**, comparing sets of official statistics to discover the social phenomena responsible for suicide rates.

Firstly, Durkheim looked at possible non-social influences on suicide such as climate, heredity, alcoholism and mental illness, but concluded that none of these profoundly affected the suicide rate.

After examining possible social variables, Durkheim produced the following hypothesis: 'the suicide rate varies inversely according to the degree of **social integration** and **moral regulation** of the social group of which the individual is a part.'

Types of suicide identified by Durkheim

Egoistic suicide results from a lack of social integration. Durkheim believed that people who commit egoistic suicide do not feel a strong sense of community. They suffer from an 'excess of individualism'. Durkheim suggested that some people were better integrated into society because of religious and family influences.

Durkheim noted that Catholic societies have lower suicide rates than Protestant societies. He concluded that this is because Catholics feel a stronger sense of community than Protestants. Durkheim claimed that Catholics have a stronger sense of their religious identity and their place within the Catholic community, whereas the Protestant encouragement of 'free will' means that Protestants are not as committed to their religious community.

He also noted that suicide rates showed that married people with children are more protected from suicide than single or divorced people or childless couples. Durkheim suggested that the protection comes not from marriage itself, but from the integrating effects of family life and children.

Essential notes

Durkheim believed that a key symptom of **anomie** was a high or increasing suicide rate. He therefore hoped to show that suicide was somehow connected to the failure of social mechanisms to integrate and regulate the behaviour of individuals, thus confirming a key functionalist idea – that there is a functional relationship between weak value consensus, social order and deviance.

Essential notes

The comparative method is carried out in the mind of the sociologist. It is a natural experiment, as the researcher does not experiment on real people, but relies on comparing statistics that have already been collected in order to discover correlations and possible cause and effect relationships.

Examiners' notes

This is the most common type of suicide, so you will need to deal with it in some detail.

Examiners' notes

You should know the strengths and weaknesses of the comparative method and official statistics in case the Research in Context question focuses on Durkheim's methodology.

Another thing Durkheim observed was that suicide rates tended to decline in times of war or political upheaval. This is because more individuals identify themselves with a 'common cause'. They become more patriotic and nationalistic, and therefore more integrated into collective life and, at least temporarily, less vulnerable to suicide.

Altruistic suicide is the opposite of egoistic suicide. It is caused by the over-integration of the individual into the social group. In altruistic suicide, the individual's ego, rather than being too great, is too weak to resist the demands of society, so that the individual feels he or she must commit suicide. Recent examples of such suicides include suicide bombers and the mass suicides committed by religious sects such as 'Peoples Temple'.

Anomic suicide arises from the lack of regulation of the individual by society. For example, in times of rapid economic change, individuals might find themselves in radically changed circumstances. A wealthy person who has suddenly become poor because of, for example, a stock market crash, may not be able to cope with the new set of norms and values he or she must deal with. The confusion or anomie experienced can result in suicidal action.

Fatalistic suicide results from the over-regulation of the individual, for example, in a prison or psychiatric institution.

Other functionalist theories of suicide

Maurice Halbwachs adds **urbanization** to the factors that are likely to reduce social integration and sense of community, and increase social isolation and potential suicidal action. He points out that city life is often impersonal and lacking in community spirit compared with rural communities, which are usually close-knit and well-integrated.

Jack Gibbs and Walter Martin attempted to modernize Durkheim's hypothesis by suggesting that 'the suicide rate varies inversely with the degree of status integration in the population'.

Criticism of Durkheim's theory of suicide

Despite the modifications of Halbwachs, Durkheim's theory has been subject to criticism:

- It has been suggested that suicide statistics collected between 1840 and 1870 are not reliable because there was no systematic medical examination of the dead in many parts of Europe until the late 19th century.
- Durkheim failed to explain why suicide is the most likely result of not enough or too much integration – why not some other course of action such as crime?
- Durkheim did not offer any guidance on how to recognize different types of suicide. Interpretivist sociologists note that without knowing the intention of the deceased, it is difficult to use Durkheim's classification.

Essential notes

Gibbs and Martin suggested that people's statuses usually complement each other and integrate us into society. For example, there should be no clash between being a wife and a doctor. But statuses can also cause conflict. For example, a woman doctor may feel tension between the role of doctor and the roles of wife and mother, resulting in family breakdown. Such tensions between statuses can cause social isolation, thus increasing suicide potential.

Examiners' notes

Durkheim's concepts – especially social integration, egoism, excessive individualism and anomie – are vague and therefore difficult to operationalize, test and measure – to convert into a quantifiable research method.

☞ This topic continues on the next two pages

Interpretivist theories of suicide

Interpretivist sociologists such as J. D. Douglas and J. Maxwell Atkinson have questioned the reliability and validity of suicide statistics, and are critical of Durkheim's hypothesis that suicide rates are the product of social integration and moral regulation.

The social and cultural meanings of suicide

Douglas argues that the suicide rate is not an objective fact waiting to be discovered, as Durkheim assumes. He argues that in order to understand how the suicide rate has come about we must examine the **cultural meanings** that are attached to suicide in different societies. Douglas raises two key points:

1. Societies do not share the same meaning of suicide. For example, in some societies, such as Japan, suicidal action is regarded as positive or honourable. In others, such as European societies, it is regarded as morally wrong. Therefore people's potential for suicide will, to some extent, depend on the societal interpretation of suicide.
2. Douglas suggests that the more integrated a community is, the more likely it will be that a higher proportion of suicide will be covered up rather than prevented. These societies tend to interpret suicide as wrong and shameful, so relatives and friends may go to great lengths to hide evidence of suicide. Douglas therefore argues that social integration influences the recording of a death as suicide, and not the decision to kill oneself.

The study of coroners

Atkinson is critical of Durkheim's use of official statistics. He argues that suicide statistics are socially constructed – the end product of a complex set of interactions and interpretations involving victims, doctors, friends and relatives of the deceased and, significantly, coroners.

Atkinson specifically focuses on the role of coroners. These are legal officers whose function is to investigate suspicious death. Atkinson notes that officially a death is not a suicide until it has been labelled as such by a coroner's court.

The role of the coroner

When investigating suspicious death, the coroner can use five possible verdicts. If the cause of death is not due to natural causes the coroner may conclude that death was caused by misadventure (accidental death), homicide or suicide. The 'open' verdict is used if evidence is insufficient to allow him or her to come to a definite conclusion.

Atkinson observed coroner's courts and interviewed coroners. He found that they aim to uncover suicidal intent by looking for primary and secondary suicidal cues. Primary cues include suicide notes, mode of death and location of death. However, these are not clear indicators of intent to die. Only a minority of suicides leave notes, many of which are vague and ambiguous in content. Some types of deaths are clearly suicidal but others, particularly drug overdoses, are open to interpretation. Some locations are notorious suicide spots and so a death in a particular place may be a clue to

Essential notes

P. McCarthy and D. Walsh (1975) studied the suicide rate in Catholic Dublin between 1964 and 1968 and estimated that the suicide rate should have been four times greater than official records showed. They argue that family members, police officers, family doctors and court officials collaborated to cover up suicides and have them categorized as accidents due to the stigma associated with suicide in Catholic society, which regarded it as a mortal sin.

Essential notes

Note that Atkinson is interested in how the dead person interacts with others, prior to suicide and afterwards. He is also interested in how the powerful coroner interacts with the relatives, friends and colleagues of the deceased, and how he or she interprets the cues left behind by the deceased in order to label the death using the legal categories available.

intent to die. However, Atkinson notes that primary cues in themselves are insufficient to prove suicidal intent.

The coroner requires extra evidence in the form of secondary cues, which are looked for in the deceased's life history and state of mind prior to death. Atkinson argues that dominant cultural meanings of suicide (that it is caused by despair and great unhappiness) influence coroners.

Atkinson notes that details of the deceased's life history or state of mind (and therefore, whether they are unhappy or not) often come from negotiation with relatives, who may attempt to influence the coroner's verdict.

Key study

Steve Taylor and deaths on the London Underground

Research by Steve Taylor (1982), based on interviews with coroners and their officers and observation of inquests, found that coroners see breakdowns in personal relationships, unemployment, history of both mental and physical illness, and coming from a broken home as important aspects of unhappiness.

Taylor investigated 32 deaths under London Underground trains in 1982, where the mode and scene of death were identical and no suicide notes were left. Only 17 of these were eventually labelled as suicide. On observation of the inquests, Taylor concluded that suicide verdicts were not returned on the other 15 because relatives influenced the coroner's interpretation of secondary cues.

The open verdict

Atkinson has particularly drawn attention to the unreliability and invalidity of suicide statistics by examining the use of the open verdict in the UK. He carried out a social **experiment**, in which he gave the same suicidal cues to English and Danish coroners and asked them to decide on a verdict. Danish coroners tended to be more rigorous in their scrutiny of the evidence, as the open verdict does not exist in their judicial system. English coroners were much more likely to declare an open verdict.

In conclusion, then, both Atkinson and Taylor suggest that we cannot take suicide statistics at face value as Durkheim did. We must look at the way such statistics are socially constructed. It may be that the official suicide statistics tell us more about the ways in which they are collected and interpreted by coroners than they tell us about the causes of suicide.

Examiners' notes

Suicide notes are a type of expressive document and secondary data (see p 73). Some sociologists use mass media reports to investigate possible reasons for suicide. Be aware too that mass reports, in print or visual form, have been cited as a possible cause of suicide. Some sociologists are interested in how social networking sites may fuel suicide patterns.

Examiners' notes

Both Atkinson and Taylor use a form of **non-participant observation** or direct observation (see pp 79–80). Make sure you are able to identify the strengths and weaknesses of this method in the context of coroner's inquests.

Examiners' notes

Atkinson used a social experiment to compare British and Danish coroners. Make sure you are able to clearly differentiate this type of experiment from other types. Also be aware of its strengths and weaknesses as a method.

Functionalism and consensus theory

Functionalism is very much associated with American sociology from roughly the 1930s to the 1960s, but its origins lie in the work of French sociologist Émile Durkheim, at the end of the 19th century.

Durkheim argued that crime and deviance can only be explained by looking at the way societies are socially organized – at their social structures. Functionalism is therefore a structuralist theory.

Structuralist theories are generally also positivist theories. This means that they see human behaviour as being shaped by social forces, or social facts, beyond the control of the individual. In other words, people behave the way they do because the social forces bearing down on them propel them (possibly against their will) in a particular direction.

Functionalism sees society as being a social system that is made up of inter-dependent social institutions such as family, education, the political system, the criminal justice system and religion. Functionalists often use a biological analogy to describe how society works, likening it to the human body, with all its organs working together to bring about good health – just as all the social institutions of society work together to bring about social order.

Functionalists argue that capitalist societies are generally characterized by social order. According to functionalism, social order is dependent on four social processes.

1. Successful socialization into value consensus

Members of society learn the basic norms and values of society during primary socialization that occurs in the family. For example, children learn the difference between right and wrong and appropriate gender roles from their parents.

Secondary agents of socialization such as education systems are vital in that they transmit shared cultural values to produce conformity and consensus. Durkheim believed that subjects such as history, language and religious education link the individual to society, past and present, by promoting a sense of pride in the historical and religious achievements of their nation. Talcott Parsons argued that the main function of education was to act as a social bridge between the family unit and wider society. Education also socializes children into values such as achievement, competition and individualism – functionalists see the transmission of these values as essential in preparing young people for the world of work.

Durkheim argued that the major function of religion is to socialize society's members into value consensus by investing certain values with a sacred quality, by infusing them with religious symbolism and special significance. Therefore these values become **moral codes** – beliefs that society agrees to revere and socialize children into. Such codes regulate our social behaviour with regard to crime, sexual behaviour and obligation to others.

Essential notes

Functionalism is a macro theory, in that it is more interested in how society and the social institutions that make up society determine people's behaviour. It is not that interested in finding out how people feel about these structural influences.

Essential notes

Functionalism is sometimes called consensus theory because of the emphasis on socialization into shared values, norms and traditions, creating consensus and conformity.

Essential notes

Durkheim's study of suicide highlights the role of social integration in people's potential to kill themselves.

2. Social integration

This refers to people's sense of belonging to society or a community. Socialization agencies such as education function to bring about a sense of social integration through the teaching of, for example, history and religion. The mass media may create the conditions for social integration by promoting nationalism or by creating moral panics. Religion creates moral communities, which people identify with; for example, Christian, Muslim or Jewish.

3. Social control

Once members of society have been socialized into values, they need to be regulated morally by having their values reinforced by informal agencies of control such as the family; for example; through praise and punishment, and religion; for example, through promises of heaven and threats of hell. Formal agencies of control such as the criminal justice system; for example, police, the law, the judiciary and fear of imprisonment, also encourage people to conform.

4. Members of society are encouraged to take their place in the specialized division of labour as workers

Education encourages learning skills and attitudes through exams and qualifications, so that we can work in jobs that suit our abilities; families encourage us to commit to a career.

However, Durkheim argues that value consensus is weaker in modern industrial societies because the complexity of modern life, especially urban life, has undermined the authority of religion and the family. Durkheim argued that city dwellers were more likely to experience anomie (moral confusion), meaning that they are less committed to society's rules and laws and therefore more likely to engage in actions that challenge value consensus such as crime and deviance.

Evaluation of functionalism

- It is **over deterministic**, suggesting that behaviour is wholly determined by social factors. It does not consider choice or the interpretations of individuals.
- It presents an over-socialized picture of people being turned into conformist citizens. However some people may resist this process.
- It fails to account for the social conflict that exists in modern societies, placing too much emphasis on consensus and order, although Durkheim's concept of anomie did anticipate the potential for social conflict.
- It fails to consider possible social dysfunctions such as the domestic violence that occurs in some families.

Essential notes

Specialized division of labour refers to all jobs in society that ensure order and stability. All workers, however skilled or unskilled, play a major role in ensuring that society works efficiently. Imagine life without, for example, trained doctors, sewage workers, electricians, supermarket workers or cleaners.

Examiners' notes

In 33-mark essay questions you may be asked to assess the contribution of functionalism to our understanding of the way society is organized. Remember to summarize and evaluate functionalism if the Theory and Method exam question focuses on structuralist or macro theories. When evaluating, try to contrast functionalism with Marxism, social action theory and postmodernism.

Marxism and conflict theory

Marxism is a structuralist theory in that it argues that the organization or structure of capitalist society, especially the fact that such societies are based on social class relationships, is the main influence on social behaviour.

Marxism sees capitalist society as organized into two interdependent parts. The infrastructure is the economic system – the way society produces goods. In capitalist societies, goods are manufactured mainly in factories. This production involves a relationship between two economic classes – the bourgeoisie or capitalist class owns the means of production (land, factories and machines). The **proletariat** or working class hires out its labour power (its skills and strength) to the capitalist class in return for a wage.

The relationship between these two classes is unequal and is based on conflict because the bourgeoisie aim to extract maximum labour at the lowest cost. As a result, the bourgeoisie exploit the labour of the working class, especially because the value of labour when sold as a product is worth more than the wage paid. This **surplus value** is pocketed by the capitalist class and is the basis of vast profits made by many employers. These profits are responsible for the great inequalities in wealth and income between the ruling and working classes.

The second part of the capitalist social system – the superstructure – is made up of social institutions such as the family, education and mass media. Marxists argue that capitalist societies are inherently unstable because of the potential for conflict between the social classes. The function of the superstructure is to reproduce the values and ideas of the ruling class (known as ideology) so that the working class are unaware of the conflicts of interest that divide them from the capitalist class. The working class therefore accept their unequal position in society as natural and inevitable. This **false class-consciousness** ensures that working-class conformity and class inequalities in areas such as income, education and health are reproduced generation after generation.

Marxists are therefore suggesting that working-class behaviour is constrained and shaped by the class inequality that characterizes the infrastructure. However, Karl Marx believed that workers would eventually become politically conscious of capitalist inequality and exploitation and collectively take revolutionary action against the capitalist class.

Evaluation of Marxism
- It is argued that Marxism may put too much emphasis on conflict. Capitalism has improved the standard of living of the working class, who may be aware of inequality and exploitation but feel that their improved standard of living compensates for this. They may therefore actively choose to carry on cooperating with capitalism because it has benefitted them in terms of economic standards, education, welfare and health care.
- Marxism has also been criticized for **economic reductionism** –

reducing behaviour to class relationships. Marxists may neglect the fact that social behaviour can also be influenced by religious, patriarchal, nationalistic and ethnic structures and relationships.

- Marx's description of capitalism and its inevitable move towards revolution has simply not occurred. Indeed, capitalism has grown stronger and, through globalization, has spread across the world.
- Marx predicted a **polarization** of people in capitalist society into a tiny rich minority and an extremely poor majority, but this has not occurred. There are great wealth and income inequalities, but there has also been massive middle-class growth, which Marx did not anticipate.

Neo-Marxism

Louis Althusser focused on the role of the state and argued that it was composed of two elements: repressive state apparatuses composed of the coercive institutions such as the police and the army, and ideological state apparatuses such as the education system, the mass media and religion, which socialize the working class into passive acceptance of their lot and, consequently, false class-consciousness. Herbert Marcuse argues that our wants, needs and desires are manipulated by the media and especially advertising, to increase profits by selling even more capitalist commodities. Marcuse argues that the function of the media is to ensure that the minds of the masses are focused on trivial entertainment rather than any critical analysis of capitalism.

Some Neo-Marxists are critical of the economic determinism of traditional Marxism. They argue that social behaviour is not always shaped by the economic system. Antonio Gramsci believed that ideas could exist independently of both the infrastructure and the superstructure, which could challenge the hegemony or cultural dominance of the bourgeoisie. These ideas have been developed by the 'New Criminology' (see pp 20–21) which sees criminal behaviour as a form of political resistance to capitalist inequality and Marxist subcultural theory (see p 21), which sees youth cultures as a form of symbolic resistance to capitalism.

However, David Harvey notes that in the past 20 years capitalism has gone through major organizational changes. He notes that globalization has helped to create whole new areas of commerce and thus new sources of profit. In particular, transnational corporations are exploiting the labour power of developing nations to produce cheap goods for marketing in the affluent West. He suggests that states are now less powerful than global institutions such as transnationals and the World Trade Organization. Finally, Harvey argues that social class as the dominant source of inequality is likely to be replaced by divisions linked to gender, ethnicity, religion, and even alternative political movements such as the green movement.

Examiners' notes

In 33-mark essay questions, you may be asked to assess the contribution of Marxism to our understanding of the way society is organized. Remember to summarize and evaluate Marxism if the Theory and Method exam question focuses on structuralist, conflict or macro theories. When evaluating Marxism, try to contrast it with functionalism, social action theory and postmodernism.

Essential notes

Neo-Marxists are influenced by interpretivism, and so are interested in how people interpret social class, exploitation and inequality. The Centre for Contemporary Cultural Studies (CCCS) examined how young working-class spectacular youth cultures can be seen to resist the cultural dominance of the bourgeoisie through their use of fashion and music (see p 21).

Feminism

Feminism focuses on the conflict between men and women and the social structure of patriarchy (male domination, female subordination and therefore gender inequality) that characterizes the organization of modern societies. It focuses on gender inequalities in education and employment, social mobility, political power and family relationships. Broadly speaking, there are three types of feminism.

1. Liberal feminism

Liberal feminists see society as patriarchal but suggest that women's opportunities are improving because of the **feminization of the economy** (the **service sector** has become dominated by a female workforce), improved educational achievement and a radical change in social attitudes that Helen Wilkinson calls a **genderquake**. She notes that the aspirations of the present female generation are radically different from those of their mothers and grandmothers. The current generation are not content to accept that their lives should be solely defined and shaped by domestic and family roles, and so are more demanding with regard to educational and career ambitions. They see themselves as equals to men.

Liberal feminists also note that marriage has become more egalitarian because women now have reproductive rights (with access to contraceptives and abortion, which allows them to control their fertility), divorce and economic power derived from better wages. Furthermore, they argue that gender-role socialization in families is slowly changing in favour of females, as girls are no longer viewed as second class citizens or encouraged to see themselves as subordinate to males. Liberal feminists are optimistic about the future of females in modern societies.

2. Marxist feminism

Marxist feminists such as Margaret Benston see patriarchy as an ideological aspect of capitalism. They argue that the bourgeoisie uses gender to divide and rule the male and female working class. Patriarchal ideology transmits the idea that women are inferior or subordinate to men and this makes it easier for capitalism to control and exploit men and women.

Benston argues that capitalism transmits the idea that women's family role as mothers and housewives is their most important function because women's domestic labour is crucial to capitalism in two important respects. First, capitalism requires a future workforce – it is the role of the mother-housewife to reproduce and to bring up the future workforce free of charge for the capitalist class. Second, the present workforce requires maintenance – it needs to be fed and its batteries recharged to be efficient. The housewife role maintains the health and efficiency of the male workforce at no extra cost to the capitalist class.

Other Marxist feminists see women as part of the **reserve army of labour**, which is only hired by capitalist enterprises in times of rapid economic expansion, and fired when recession sets in. Marxists argue that women are vulnerable to trends such as economic recession, downsizing and mergers, and so make up a more disposable part of the workforce.

3. Radical feminism

Radical feminists such as Christine Delphy argue that gender inequality is more important than class inequality. They argue that society is divided into two basic gender classes – men and women – whose interests are opposed. Modern societies are patriarchal societies, in which men exploit and oppress women in all aspects of social life. Culture, government, tradition, religion, law, education and the media all reflect patriarchal ideology and power.

All these types of patriarchal inequality originate, not in wider society, but in the intimacy of personal relationships, and especially in the gender-role socialization found in families. Radical feminists note that patriarchal ideology is used to control women for the benefit of men. Women are told how to look, dress and behave. When patriarchal ideology fails, then women are always under the threat of male violence and sexual aggression, which limits their capacity to live as free and independent beings.

Evaluation of feminism

- Like functionalism and Marxism, feminism is over deterministic – it suggests that social behaviour is wholly determined by social factors. It does not take choice or how females interpret their social situation into consideration. Catherine Hakim notes that some women may be happy to be mothers and housewives.
- It presents an over-socialized picture of women being turned into conformist mothers or housewives. In this sense, Marxist and radical feminism are outdated and fail to consider recent changes such as genderquake, educational success or new jobs for women.
- Marxist feminists believe that **domestic labour** benefits capitalism but Sylvia Walby (1986) is critical of this approach. She argues that women staying at home harms capitalism, as women competing with men for jobs could lower wages and increase profits. Women who earn also have superior spending power, which boosts capitalism.
- The reserve army of labour theory fails to explain why there are men's jobs and women's jobs and why women ended up with responsibility for domestic labour.
- Feminism neglects the influence of social class and ethnicity. Middle-class women may not be exploited by men as much as working-class women because they have more access to economic power. The influence of factors such as religion or racism could mean that black or Asian women experience more exploitation than white women. These criticisms have led to what has become known as **difference feminism**.

Examiners' notes

Use examples from other areas of the specification to illustrate these ideas. For example, you could look at the lack of women in top jobs or in politics, or at the way women are represented in the mass media or in world religions.

Examiners' notes

In 33-mark essay questions, you may be asked to assess the contribution of feminism to our understanding of the way society is organized. Note that you will need to summarize and evaluate feminism if the Theory and Method question focuses on patriarchal, conflict or macro theories. Remember to discuss why feminist sociologists prefer certain methods (see p 48). When evaluating feminism, try to contrast it with functionalism, Marxism, social action theory and postmodernism.

Social action theory

Social action theorists, or interactionist sociologists, reject the assumption held by functionalist and Marxist sociologists – that social behaviour is constrained and even made predictable by the organization of society. Social action theorists see people as having a much more proactive role in shaping social life.

Social action theorists reject the view that people's behaviour is the product of external forces over which they have little control. Chris Brown argues that people engage in voluntary behaviour. Most people do not feel themselves to be the puppets of society.

However, although people operate as individuals, they are aware of other people around them. Social action theorists argue that the attitudes and actions of others influence the way people think and behave. Social action theorists also argue that society is the product of people interacting in social groups and trying to make sense of their own and each other's behaviour.

People are able to work out what is happening in any given situation because they bring a set of interpretations to every **social interaction** and use them to make sense of social behaviour. In particular, people apply meanings to symbolic behaviour. When they interact with others, they are on the lookout for symbols, because these give clues as to how the other person is interpreting their behaviour. For example, smiling is symbolic behaviour that might be interpreted as social approval.

Experience of **symbolic interaction** results in people acquiring knowledge about what is appropriate behaviour in particular situations. They learn that particular contexts demand particular social responses. For example, drinking and dancing at a party is regarded as appropriate, yet the same behaviour at a funeral is inappropriate.

Socialization and identity

Social action theorists argue that socialization involves learning a stock of shared interpretations and meanings for most given social interactions. Families, for example, teach children how to interact with and interpret the actions of others.

Social action theorists suggest that socialization results in individuals acquiring a social identity, which refers to the personality characteristics and qualities that particular cultures associate with certain social roles or groups. In British culture, for example, mothers are expected to be loving, nurturing and selfless, so women who are mothers will attempt to live up to this description and acquire this social identity. As children grow up, socialization and interaction with others will show them what British culture expects of them in terms of obligations, duties and behaviour towards others.

Furthermore, the individual has a subjective sense of her or his uniqueness and identity. Sociologists call this the **self**. It is partly the product of what others think is expected of a person's social identity. However, 'self' is also the product of how the individual interprets her or his experience and life history. For example, some women may have, in their own minds, serious misgivings about their role as mother. The self, then, is the link between what society expects from a particular role and the individual's interpretation of whether she or he is living up to that role successfully.

The concept of self has been explored extensively by social action sociologists. Some have suggested that the self has two parts – the 'I' and the 'me'. The 'I' is the private inner self, whereas the 'me' is the social self that participates in everyday interaction. When a person plays a social role as a teacher or student, the 'me' is in action. The 'me' is shaped by the reactions of others – that is, people act in ways they think are socially desirable. However, the 'I' supplies the confidence or self-esteem to play the role successfully.

Key study

Erving Goffman (1959) argues that social interaction is about successful **role-playing**.

He suggests that we are all social actors engaged in the drama of everyday life. Stage directions are symbolized by the social and cultural context in which the action takes place. For example, the classroom as a stage symbolizes particular rules that must be followed if the interaction is to be successful. For example, students sit at desks while teachers can move around the room freely.

Labelling theory is a type of social action theory, which points out that although there is a consensus of meaning on how people should behave, it is constantly evolving and changing. For example, interactionists argue there is no such thing as 'right' or 'wrong' behaviour. However, some groups have more power and are able to impose their meanings or interpretations on the rest of us. They make the rules (for example, laws), which define the behaviour of other groups as deviant or criminal. They are able to apply negative labels via the mass media (via moral panics), education (for example, the ideal student stereotype) and through the legal system (for example, the police use of stereotypes of the typical criminal or suspicious person). Interactionists point out that labels, applied by means of education or policing, have a powerful effect on the self-esteem and status of groups such as ethnic minorities and can bring about self-fulfilling prophecies and deviant subcultural responses.

Evaluation social action theory

- The main weakness of social action theory lies in its failure to explore the wider social factors that create the context in which symbols, self and interaction all exist, for example, class and patriarchy. This means that it has no explanation for where the symbolic meanings originate.
- It also completely fails to explore power differences between groups and individuals, and why these might occur. For example, Marxists argue that the capitalist class is able to impose its interpretations of reality on less powerful groups in society.

Examiners' notes

In the Theory and Method essay questions, you may be asked to assess the contribution of social action theory to our understanding of the way society is organized. You should summarize and evaluate social action theory if the question focuses on interactionist, interpretivist or micro theories. When evaluating social action theory, try to contrast it with functionalism, Marxism and postmodernism.

Modernity and postmodernity

Postmodernists argue that the history of British society can be divided into two broad periods. The 20th century was dominated by the modern industrial period – modern society. However, towards the latter end of the 20th century – the 1980s – society began to evolve into the postmodern period. The two periods differ from each other in important ways.

The modern or industrial period was characterized by six key features:

1. Industrialization was organized along capitalist lines. Mainly, people were employed in heavy industries such as coal, iron and steel and shipbuilding, or in factories, manufacturing products such as cars, textiles and electrical items.
2. Social class was the major source of most people's identity in that the capitalist ruling class owned the factories, the middle classes managed them and the working class worked in them. Generally, people were proud to identify themselves using class labels, and differences in values and lifestyles were clearly class differences.
3. Urbanization resulted, as industrialization saw mass migration from rural areas to the urban centres in search of factory work.
4. The state or government extended its influence over a range of aspects of people's lives. In modern society, the government takes responsibility for the education, health and welfare of people from the cradle to the grave.
5. Scientific or rational thinking became more important than irrational belief systems such as religion. The modernist theory of positivism argues that the scientific approach is the only approach to take in solving society's problems and improving living standards.
6. Big ideas or **meta-narratives** developed – for example, political theories such as Socialism, as well as sociological theories such as functionalism, Marxism and feminism – in order to explain how modern society works. For example, in the 19th century, positivist sociology developed as a subject, which aimed to explain the modern industrial world scientifically.

However, postmodernists believe that the modern world is dissolving and being replaced with postmodern ideas and institutions.

Distinguishing the postmodern world from the modern world

This postmodern world has various characteristics that distinguish it from the modern world.

- The nature of work has dramatically changed – the primary sector (such as coal mining) and secondary sectors (such as factory work) of the economy have declined. The service sector, which involves processing information (such as working in offices, schools or for the government) and servicing consumption (such as working in a shop), has become the dominant sector of the economy. There are now more university lecturers than coal miners in the UK.
- As a result of these changes in the economy, social class as the major source of identity has allegedly gone into decline.

- Postmodern societies are 'media-saturated' societies – magazines, television, cinema, pop music and the internet have all become central to the way we live our lives. As a result, popular culture now shapes personal identity.
- Globalization is also a norm in postmodern societies. This means that we are now more exposed to, for example, global brands, icons, music, films, food and drink than ever before. This combination of media saturation and globalization means that people have more choices available to them in terms of constructing identity.
- The consumption of consumer goods, especially conspicuous consumption of designer goods, is increasingly an important aspect of personal identity.
- The modernist meta-narratives such as science, socialism and feminism have lost their power and influence as explanations of how society works. For example, people have become sceptical, even cynical, about the power of science to change the world, as many of the world's problems are seen to have been caused by science and technology.
- Postmodernists now argue that there is no such thing as 'truth' – all knowledge is relative and has something to contribute to our understanding of how society works. Sociology, therefore, is only one set of ideas that must compete with others.

Evaluation of postmodernism

- Critics of postmodernism argue that it probably exaggerates the degree of economic and social change; for example, the majority of workers in the UK still work in the manufacturing industry.
- Evidence suggests that social class is still important as a source of identity – surveys indicate that people still see social class as a strong subjective influence in their lives.
- Postmodernists ignore the fact that the nature of people's consumption – what and how much they consume – still very much depends on their income, which depends on the job they have, in other words, their social class.
- People's ability to make choices is also still influenced by factors stressed by modernists such as gender and ethnicity, for example.
- Women are still paid on average 80% of men's earnings and still have to negotiate a glass ceiling in their attempt to get access to top jobs, while ethnic minorities still face the daily experience of racism in all its shapes and forms.

Essential notes

Illustrate these ideas using examples from across the specification. For example, postmodern ideas on religion suggest that the power of world religions to impose a collective religious identity on groups of people is in decline. Globalization and the increasing relativity of 'truth' mean that people increasingly 'pick and mix' their religious identity in a religious marketplace.

Examiners' notes

In 33-mark essay questions you may be asked to assess the evolution of Western societies from modern to postmodern. Note that you should summarize and evaluate modernist and postmodernist theories, and try to illustrate modernism by referring to modernist theories such as functionalism and Marxism.

Positivist research methods

Positivists are very influenced by the natural sciences. Natural scientists such as biologists, physicists and chemists have shown us that plants, animals and chemicals behave in predictable ways because of natural laws. For example, water obeys certain physical laws when boiled or frozen. Positivist sociologists have adapted and applied these ideas to human behaviour, arguing that we should treat people as objects whose behaviour can be observed and counted in the same way as animals, the weather and chemical elements.

Positivists see human behaviour as the product of the organization of the society in which we live. Positivists argue that the structure of society produces social laws over which we have no control or choice and which determine our behaviour; they see people as the puppets of society. Positivists argue that social behaviour is patterned, in that groups of people behave in similar, and therefore predictable, ways.

Positivists believe that sociology should adopt the research methods of the natural sciences to research human behaviour, and that:

- Sociologists should study only what they can objectively see, measure and count.
- Research subjects should be exposed to standardized stimuli under controlled conditions.
- Reliability should be high – another sociologist should be able to use the method to repeat the research and get the same results.
- Research methods should produce quantifiable or statistical data.
- Statistical relationships (that is, correlations) can be established between various factors, which, if confirmed, can be classified as 'social laws' that explain the causes of patterned social behaviour.

Experiments

In many of the natural sciences, the laboratory experiment is the main means by which scientists gather data and test theories.

Scientists like experiments because they are conducted in a controlled environment. In a laboratory experiment, the researcher is interested in the relationship between an **independent variable** (a possible cause) and a **dependent variable** (a possible effect). The experiment involves setting up two identical groups – an **experimental group** and a **control group** – which are treated differently. The experimental group is exposed to the independent variable and its behaviour is often compared to the control group (which is not exposed) to monitor any differences between the two. Any differences are seen as dependent variables or effects.

Positivists regard the laboratory experiment as reliable for three reasons:

1. The original researcher can control the conditions and specify the precise steps that were used in the original experiment, so others can easily repeat the steps to re-run it.
2. It produces quantitative data, so the results of the re-run experiment can be compared to the original easily.
3. It is a detached and objective method – the researcher merely manipulates the variables and records the results.

Evaluating laboratory experiments

There are practical, ethical and theoretical reasons why sociologists are not keen on using laboratory experiments.

- Humans are complex beings, so it is impossible to construct identical human experimental and control groups. No two humans are exactly alike, which means we experience and interpret all social situations in different ways.
- Laboratory experiments can only focus on small samples and so are not that useful in studying large-scale social phenomena.
- A laboratory experiment is an artificial environment and any behaviour that occurs in it may be a product of the environment. The subjects may act differently; for example, they may feel self-important, anxious or resentful, or they may work out what the researcher wants and give it to them. This is the **Hawthorne effect**, named after experiments conducted by Mayo in the 1920s at the Hawthorne factory in the USA where it was first observed.
- Experiments may result in harming subjects. For example, exposing children to violent films for long periods may do psychological or emotional damage.
- Interpretivists argue that humans are fundamentally different from other natural phenomena. We have free will and choice. Our behaviour is not 'caused' by external forces, so it cannot be explained in terms of cause and effect relationships.

Positivists prefer research methods that produce data in numerical form. They also like to use secondary data such as official statistics, collected by government sources.

Social surveys

A social survey involves collecting the same type of data from many people, usually via questionnaires or, less often, structured interviews.

Some surveys consist of **longitudinal research**, which involves studying the same group of people over a long period of time. These provide a clear image of changes in attitudes and behaviour over time, but can be problematic, as respondents may drop out or researchers may lose track of them. The views of those that remain in the sample may also be significantly different from the views of those who drop out, so over time the sample may become increasingly unrepresentative.

Questionnaires

A questionnaire is simply a list of questions that are written down in advance. They are the main method for gathering data in social surveys. They are handed out or posted to the respondent – the person chosen by the researcher to answer the questions. This type of questionnaire is known as a self-completion questionnaire. Other questionnaires become interview schedules, in that they are read out and filled in on behalf of the respondent by trained interviewers. This type of questionnaire is known as a formal or structured interview.

When constructing a questionnaire, the sociologist must ensure that the right questions are asked to unearth the exact information that is needed.

Examiners' notes

The laboratory experiment is regarded as the ultimate methodology by positivists, so you could use the arguments about the strengths and weaknesses of this method in 33-mark Theory and Method exam questions that ask you to examine the positivist versus interpretivist debate.

Essential notes

Surveys generally aim to find out facts about a population or uncover differences in beliefs or social attitudes or test a hypothesis. For example, every 10 years, the government conducts the census, aimed at every household in the UK – to uncover facts about British lifestyles.

Examiners' notes

You should know some strengths and weaknesses of longitudinal surveys, as they tend to be asked in short exam questions. Also, think about how such surveys might be used to study crime and deviance.

Examiners' notes

It is important to clearly define what is meant by a questionnaire and to explain how they are usually organized.

☞ This topic continues on the next two pages

Essential notes

It is important to conduct a **pilot survey**, to resolve possible questionnaire problems. This entails testing the questions on a small group of people who share the characteristics of the main sample. A pilot survey is useful to check that the questions are clear and do not upset or lead the participants, that the sampling technique used will target the 'right' types of people to fill in the questionnaire, that the researchers are well trained and that the data produced is the kind that is wanted.

Essential notes

Some questionnaires use attitudinal scales and ask respondents for their views on a scale of 1 to 5, with 1 as 'strongly agree', 3 as 'neutral' and 5 as 'strongly disagree'.

Essential notes

Positivists regard questionnaire surveys as scientific, as they are standardized, objective, reliable and collect mainly quantitative data, which can be compared easily for correlations. There are few ethical problems with questionnaires, especially if delivered via the post, as returning them indicates that respondents have given their consent.

Table 11
Strengths and weaknesses of questionnaires

So the questions must focus on the hypothesis. Turning the hypothesis into a series of questions is called 'operationalization'.

Ideally, questions should be objective and it is essential that they contain neutral wording. However, questions can be biased, in that they can 'lead' respondents to the answers the researcher requires. They can sometimes be 'loaded', or written in such a way that the respondent is provoked into an emotional response that seeks to evade the truth.

Questionnaires tend to use 'closed' questions with a choice of pre-set answers with accompanying tick boxes, which produce quantitative data.

Questionnaires have a number of strengths and weaknesses, as shown in this table.

Questionnaires – strengths
• If postal, can be used to reach large numbers of people around the country, which may improve the representativeness of the sample (e.g. sociologists might want to compare how people in Scotland view crime compared to people in England or Wales)
• They are less time-consuming for respondents than interviews
• Reasonably cheap compared to other methods
• Useful for research that includes sensitive or embarrassing questions, as these can be answered in the privacy of the home rather than face-to-face, which might undermine validity
• Ensure that the sociologist has minimum contact with the respondent, so reducing the possibility of the respondent feeling suspicious or threatened

Questionnaires – weaknesses
• Especially if postal, suffer from low response or even **non-response**
• Those returned may not be representative of the research population, as the replies may be from people with strong unrepresentative views
• May not be suitable for finding out why people behave the way they do, as real life is often too complex to categorize in closed questions and responses
• Respondents may interpret questions in a different way from that intended by the researcher
• Artificial devices that are not a normal part of daily reality, so people may respond with suspicion and may not tell the truth, or may be partial, as they feel threatened by the research or researchers
• By choosing the questions and responses, the researcher has already mapped out the experiences and interpretations of respondents (e.g. they may be forced to tick boxes that only approximate to their experiences, views and opinions, thus undermining the validity of the data, which may frustrate respondents and result in non-response)

Self-report questionnaires

In an attempt to uncover the true amount of crime in society, some criminologists have used a type of questionnaire called a self report. It lists various petty criminal acts and asks respondents to tick those they have committed without being caught. Sociologists attempt to improve validity by stressing confidentiality and anonymity for the respondents.

Marsh notes that validity is undermined by under-reporting and over-reporting. People may under-report because self-report studies are retrospective and depend on being able to remember crimes committed 12 months before. Some people exaggerate offences to create a 'tough' impression. Others keep quiet, as they fear that the police will be informed.

The representativeness of self-report questionnaires is questioned for three reasons:

1. It is impossible to include all criminal acts in a questionnaire. This means the researcher must be selective, which raises problems as to which offences to include or not.
2. Self reports are distributed mainly to young people – it would be difficult to get businessmen to cooperate and admit to various types of white-collar or corporate crime.
3. Josine Junger-Tas (1989) reports a sliding scale of responses to self-report questionnaires, depending on how much contact respondents have had with the criminal justice system. Response rates from people with a criminal record were lower than from those without.

Structured interviews

Positivists view structured interviews as a scientific method. These interviews usually involve the researcher reading out a list of closed questions from an interview schedule – a type of questionnaire – and ticking boxes or writing down answers according to pre-set fixed categories on behalf of the respondent. The interviewer plays a passive role, acting as a recording machine, and may not deviate from the interview schedule questions.

The British Crime Survey (BCS) used 46 983 face-to-face structured interviews with a sample of people aged 16 and over, living in private households in England and Wales. Using laptop computers, 22 trained interviewers recorded the responses.

In many ways, structured interviews are similar to questionnaires, so they share some of the same strengths, but although they share the same problems as questionnaires, some of these are unique to this method. The advantages and disadvantages are as follows.

Essential notes

Pilot surveys are essential in order to avoid this problem.

Essential notes

The danger exists that questionnaires might be completed in a group rather than by the individual alone. Responses may reflect peer group pressure rather than own views.

Essential notes

There will always be some social groups who will never respond positively to a questionnaire because they are 'deviant' and associate questionnaires with authority.

Examiners' notes

Self reports are a fertile area for exam questions, as they are a good example of the questionnaire method in action in the context of crime and deviance.

Examiners' notes

When you answer a question on structured interviews, explain clearly how they work in practice, so differentiating them from other types of interview methods. It is common for exam questions to ask candidates to compare different types of interviews.

☞ This topic continues on the next two pages

Examiners' notes

Note that you should know about random *and* non-random sampling techniques (see pp 74–75).

Essential notes

Pre-coded answers to questions mean that any later researcher will categorize answers in the same way as the original researcher, thus ensuring reliability.

Examiners' notes

Make sure you give examples of this interview bias. Use social class, gender, ethnicity or age to illustrate how power or status differences between the interviewer and interviewees might undermine the validity of the research data.

Table 12
Advantages and disadvantages of structured interviews

Structured interviews – advantages	Structured interviews – disadvantages
The focus on closed questions and fixed categories means they are very useful for collecting straightforward factual data	Inflexible, as the questionnaire or interview schedule is drawn up in advance and the interviewer must stick to it rigidly; interpretivists note that this makes it impossible to pursue interesting leads that may emerge during the interview
Can use relatively large samples, as they can be conducted fairly quickly (e.g. the BCS interviews took an average of 48 minutes per interview to complete)	Only snapshots taken at one moment in time, and so they fail to capture the dynamic changing nature of social life
The interviewer can explain the aims and objectives of the research, clarify instructions and generally make sure that informed consent has been granted	Interpretivists note that there is often a gap between what people say they do and what they actually do – they may not put their prejudices into action or they are unaware that they behave in certain ways
Better response rates than postal questionnaires, as the interviewer can return if the respondent is not at home	All interviews are interactions, so there is the danger of interview bias that the interviewee will feel that he or she lacks power or status compared to the interviewer, and may feel threatened by the research, thus giving invalid views
Regarded as scientific *and* reliable by positivist sociologists, they are standardized measuring instruments; interviewers can be trained to conduct each interview in exactly the same way (e.g. same questions, order, wording and tone of voice), and so should produce similar data	Responses may lack validity because the interviewee responds in a socially desirable way – in the way he or she believes the researcher wants, rather than providing his or her own opinion; the interviewee may therefore be partial with the truth

Secondary data – official statistics

Positivists are keen on some types of secondary data such as official statistics collected by government agencies. The most commonly available sources of official statistics are those from the Census – a questionnaire survey that is conducted every 10 years on the whole population. Official statistics have a number of strengths and weaknesses.

Official statistics – strengths

- easy and cheap to access, involving little effort on the part of the sociologist
- contemporary (e.g. the 2010 crime statistics will be published in 2011)
- usually collected in a standardized, systematic and scientific way (e.g. registration data on birth, marriage, divorce and death is highly reliable and valid because it is the outcome of long-standing, systematic procedures)
- allow us to make comparisons between groups (e.g. the census covers the whole UK population at the same time and asks everyone the same questions, making it easy to compare different groups and regions)
- trends over a period of time can be observed easily (e.g. sociologists might notice that there is less crime as people get older)
- generally regarded as representative, as they have been produced by large-scale studies, often covering the whole population

Official statistics – weaknesses

- may not present a complete picture (e.g. the government does not collect statistics relating to the socio-economic background or employment status of people who have been arrested, prosecuted or convicted and sent to prison)
- open to political abuse (e.g. they can be manipulated or 'massaged' by governments for political advantage)
- socially constructed (i.e. the end result of someone making a decision that a particular set of activities needs to be recorded and that statistics need to be collected in a particular way)
- they tell us very little about the human stories or interpretations that underpin them (e.g. crime and prison statistics tell us little about *why* people commit crime or what it feels like to be sent to prison)
- may be based on operational definitions, with which sociologists would not agree (e.g. the government often changes definitions of serious drug offences)
- Marxists argue that their ideological function is to conceal or distort reality and keep the capitalist class in power (e.g. the official crime statistics (OCS) create the impression that street crime committed by the working class is the main criminal problem in the UK, but such statistics distract society from white-collar, corporate and state crime)

Essential notes

Sociologists often use official statistics to work out the extent of a social problem so that primary research can be designed to uncover explanations. Criminologists often use the criminal statistics to work out which groups are more likely to commit crime. Durkheim used 19th century official statistics to study suicide.

Examiners' notes

Use the interpretivist arguments regarding the social construction of the criminal statistics or suicide to illustrate in depth the weaknesses of this type of secondary data.

Sampling

Sociologists who decide to use a questionnaire or structured interview survey to test a hypothesis need to think about the research population they are studying and how it should be sampled.

The **research population** – for example, if the sociologist is interested in the relationship between ethnicity and being the victim of racial attacks, decisions must be made about which ethnic minority groups will be focused on and whether the white population will also be studied, possibly as a point of comparison.

The sample – it is usually too expensive and time-consuming to ask everyone in the research population to take part in the research. Most researchers select a sample that is representative – a typical cross-section – of the population they are interested in. With a representative sample, it is possible to generalize to the wider research population – what is true of the sample should be true of the research population as a whole.

Two main sampling techniques can be used to ensure that the sample is representative of the wider research population. They are:

- random sampling
- non-random sampling.

Random sampling

A simple random sample involves selecting names randomly from a list or **sampling frame**. Using this technique, every member of the research population has an equal chance to be included in the sample, so that those chosen are likely to be a cross-section of the population.

Various types of sampling frames can be used:

- the Electoral Register (that is, a list of people over 18 years, who are registered to vote)
- the Postcode Address File
- the telephone directory
- school attendance registers
- patient records of general practitioners (GPs).

All sampling frames are unsatisfactory in some respect – they are often out of date; some groups may be over-represented, while others may not be included.

Different types of random sampling techniques

A simple random sample does not guarantee a representative sample – the researcher may, for example, end up selecting too many young people or too many males. Thus, to produce representative samples, sociologists have developed three variations on the random sample.

1. **Systematic sampling** involves randomly choosing a number between one and 10, say 'seven', and then picking out every 10th number from that number – 7, 17, 27, 37 … – on the list until the sample is complete. This does not always guarantee a representative

Essential notes

The main function of random sampling techniques is to avoid the bias that undermines the representativeness of the sample if researchers are allowed to choose who takes part in the research.

Examiners' notes

Be aware of the merits of particular sampling frames, especially those that might be used to obtain samples for the study of crime and deviance. For example, the British Crime Survey (BCS) uses the Postcode Address File to obtain a nationally representative sample of over 47000 people.

sample but the larger the sample, the more likely it is to be reasonably representative and the less likely it is to be biased.

2. **Stratified sampling** is the most common form of random sampling used in sociological research. It involves dividing the research population into a number of sampling frames, for example, by gender, age, ethnicity and social class, which represent their proportion in the research population, and then randomly selecting, say, every 10th name until the required number is reached for each sub-sample.

3. **Cluster sampling** is often used when no specific list of people is available. The researcher uses a map to randomly select a couple of areas, and then streets within those areas. The researcher then randomly targets a further sample of people or households within the streets.

Non-random sampling methods

- **Quota sampling** is often used by market research companies to target people in the street to talk about consumer products. The researcher is told by his or her company how many participants are needed in each category and goes looking for them, usually in a city centre. This sort of sampling technique is often used by television news companies and newspapers to find out people's voting preferences before an election.

- **Purposive sampling** involves researchers choosing individuals or cases that fit the nature of the research. For example, a researcher might visit a church because he or she needs to interview religious people.

- **Snowball sampling** is used mainly when it is difficult to gain access to a particular group of people because there is no sampling frame available or because they engage in deviant or illegal activities, which are normally done in isolation or in secret. This sampling technique involves finding and interviewing a person who fits the research criteria and then asking her or him to suggest someone else who might be willing to be interviewed. The sample can grow as large as the researcher wants. Martin A. Plant (1975) used this type of sampling technique in his study of cannabis use. However, this technique may not produce a representative sample, as the type of people who volunteer may differ in important respects from those who do not volunteer.

All sampling is a compromise between representativeness and practicality, and researchers often have to make do with samples that are not fully representative.

Examiners' notes

Questions on sampling are most likely to appear in the Methods in Context section of the exam paper and may focus on the merits of particular sampling frames, and random or non-random sampling techniques for the study of crime and deviance. Note that positivist survey research such as the BCS is most likely to use random sampling techniques, whereas interpretivist qualitative research is more likely to use non-random sampling techniques.

Interpretivist research methods

Interpretivists reject the positivist view that human behaviour is the product of social laws over which people have no control. They argue that we are not the puppets of society – rather, that we are the architects of society. Without people, society simply would not exist. Interpretivists also reject the view that humans can be treated like objects in much the same way as things in the natural world.

Interpretivists point out that people are active, conscious beings who act with intention and purpose. They are not propelled against their will to take certain predetermined courses of action. Instead, they make choices based on free will.

Interpretivists argue that society is the sum of people choosing to come together in social groups – known as 'social interaction'. Interpretivists point out that when people interact, they are constantly interpreting, or giving meaning to, their own behaviour and that of others. For example, a family is not just a group of people with a biological relationship – they are a group of people who interpret themselves as a family and interact accordingly. The way people interpret their parents', children's and siblings' behaviour towards themselves in turn influences their own behaviour.

Interpretivists argue that in order to understand social behaviour (and therefore, society), it is essential to discover and understand the meanings or interpretations that underpin people's actions. Interpretivist sociologists therefore stress the concept of validity – seeing the world as it really is. They argue that sociologists need to adopt sociological research methods that are ethnographic – access people's natural everyday environment. Such methods should get inside people's heads in order to see the social world through the eyes of those being studied. This is called ***verstehen*** or empathetic understanding.

Such sociologists prefer unstructured interviews, which allow people to talk at length about how they feel, and participant observation (observing behaviour by joining in their everyday activities), as these methods produce qualitative data – concerned with motives, feelings and experiences that give us first-hand insight into how people interpret the world around them. Interpretivists reject methods such as questionnaires, which they say are artificial and are unlikely to produce data that tell us how people really feel.

Field or social experiments

Interpretivists reject the use of laboratory experiments because they argue that human beings are fundamentally different from the plants, rocks and other natural phenomena that natural scientists study. Unlike these objects, we have free will and choice. Our behaviour is not 'caused' by external forces, so it cannot be explained in terms of cause and effect statements, as positivists believe.

However, interpretivists have conducted social experiments in naturally occurring settings. These **field experiments** aim to examine the way people behave in everyday, small social groups. The sociologist manipulates one particular variable, or influence, and observes the reactions of the individual or group who are being studied (and who are often not aware that a social experiment is taking place). These experiments differ from conventional laboratory experiments in that control groups are not always apparent – it is assumed that the control group is made up of similar groups who are not taking part in the experiment.

Key study

Robert Rosenthal and Lenore Jacobson (1968) manipulated teachers' expectations about students by giving them misleading information about students' abilities in order to discover what effects this would have on students' achievements.

Field experiments allow the sociologist to unravel the often hidden processes and rules of day-to-day social life, as they enable the researcher to get close to people's interpretations of everyday experiences. However, field experiments have been criticized because:

- There is often a trade-off between naturalism and control – the more natural and realistic the situation, the less control the sociologist has over variables.
- Such experiments may be unethical because they have not gained the informed consent of the participants and they often involve deception. However, interpretivist sociologists argue that deception rarely involves harm being done and that the data generated by the experiment often benefits society.
- There is a danger of a Hawthorne effect being created. For example, if a field experiment were to be conducted in a prison, any change to everyday procedures might be noticed by prisoners and guards, so their behaviour might change because of the experiment.

Unstructured interviews

An unstructured interview is like a guided conversation, in which the talk is informal but the researcher plays an active role, in that he or she manages the questions to ensure that the participant sticks to the subject of the research. The interviewer in this situation usually has a list of topics to discuss rather than an interview schedule or questionnaire. A skilful interviewer will flexibly follow up ideas, probe responses and investigate motives and feelings in ways a questionnaire can never do.

Interpretivist sociologists are keen on unstructured interviews because they are concerned with understanding the meanings or interpretations that underpin social life. They believe that unstructured interviews bring about validity through involvement, meaning that valid qualitative data can only be obtained by getting close to people's experiences and ways of thinking. The way an unstructured interview is organized stresses that what the interviewee says or thinks is the central issue – the respondent is placed at the centre of the research. By developing trust and **rapport** with the interviewee, the researcher can visualize his or her points of view – what is important and why he or she acts in a certain way.

Essential notes

In the field of criminology, field experiments are often used to test the effectiveness of social policies such as crime prevention programmes or prisoner rehabilitation, by comparing situations where a policy is being implemented with situations where it is not.

Examiners' notes

You may be asked a general question on experiments, which requires you to compare field or social experiments with laboratory experiments.

Essential notes

Unstructured interviews are useful in revealing the truth beneath the surface because they ask individuals open-ended questions about their specific experiences rather than asking the whole sample the same questions and to choose from the same set of answers.

☞ **This topic continues on the next two pages**

Essential notes

People conducting unstructured interviews should have similar social characteristics to those being interviewed, to minimize interview bias and to increase the possibility of trust.

Essential notes

Some people may be defensive and distrustful of sociological research. The higher level of rapport associated with unstructured interviews can help to overcome this barrier.

Essential notes

Unstructured interviews may be ethically problematic, as they may reveal 'guilty knowledge' – the sociologist becomes aware of crimes the respondent has committed or intends to commit.

Examiners' notes

Make sure you give examples of this interview bias. Use social class, gender, ethnicity or age to illustrate how power or status differences might undermine the validity of the research data. For example, Adams (2000) when interviewing police, dressed to look like a 'normal, law-abiding citizen', but she 'dressed down' when interviewing suspects, to avoid looking like an official person intruding into their lives.

Unstructured interviews have a number of strengths and weaknesses.

Unstructured interviews – strengths

- allow researchers to build up and modify their hypothesis during the course of the research, as new and important insights come about, either because the interviewee trusts the researcher or because the flexible nature of the interview results in unexpected information being uncovered
- some sociologists use them as a starting point to develop their initial ideas, before using more structured methods such as questionnaires
- allow the interviewer to make sure that he or she shares the same meaning as the interviewee about a particular issue, thus increasing validity
- seen as particularly suited to researching sensitive groups (i.e. people who might be suspicious of or hostile to outsiders – such as deviants or criminals)
- provide richer, more vivid and more qualitative data – the data collected often speaks for itself in the form of extensive quotations from those being interviewed

Unstructured interviews – weaknesses

- regarded as unreliable because they cannot be replicated and verified by another sociologist
- may lack objectivity because the researcher has a personal relationship with the interviewee
- practically speaking, the final research cannot contain all the information gathered and, often, the interviewer will select aspects of the interview transcript that fit the hypothesis – such selectivity may reflect the ideological biases of the researcher
- data is difficult to analyse and categorize because of the sheer volume of material in the respondent's own words
- exceptionally time-consuming to conduct and transcribe
- expensive, as training must be thorough and specialized – interviewers need to be trained in interpersonal skills so that they establish good relationships with interviewees
- all interviews are interactions and there is always the danger that the interviewee will feel that they lack power or status compared to the interviewer, so he or she may feel threatened by the research or status of the interviewer; responses may lack validity because the interviewee responds in a socially desirable way (i.e. by providing the responses they think the researcher wants or they are partial with the truth)

Personal documents

Some interpretivists use a form of secondary data known as personal or expressive documents made up of diaries, letters and autobiographies. These can be historical or contemporary, and can provide a sociologist with a rich source of qualitative data about, for example, experiences, feelings, attitudes, emotions and motives for behaviour. Sociologists are drawn to this type of data because they are a free or economical source of information, already having been gathered. They may also be used when no other source of data exists. For example, sociologists might not be able to gain access to criminal gangs but the diary or autobiography of a gang member may give us important insights into criminal behaviour.

Interpretivists like documents. They believe documents can give the researcher a valid picture of people's worldview and the meaning they apply to their actions. Documents enable sociologists to get close to people's reality. For example, suicide notes can be taken to be the final thoughts of the individual committing suicide.

However, personal documents are often very subjective, in that the writer usually wants to justify his or her actions. There may also be doubts about the **authenticity** of the document – letters and diaries can be forged. A document may lack **credibility** if it was written long after the events it describes, when key details might have been forgotten.

Positivists are not keen on documents because they regard this type of data as unreliable – it cannot be checked for accuracy by the sociologist. Documents are not standardized. For example, every person's diary is unique, even when they record the same events. Finally, the people who write personal documents may not be representative – not all sections of society keep diaries describing their behaviour. The nature of criminal activity means that criminals are less likely than other social groups to leave personal records that incriminate them and perhaps lead to their prosecution.

Observation

Interpretivist sociologists argue that observation gives first-hand insight into how people interpret the social world around them. It allows sociologists to record behaviour by observing people's actions on a daily basis. Consequently, they see the world through the eyes of the group they are observing.

Essentially, there are two types of observation.

1. Non-participant or direct observation

This has been used extensively in the field of criminal justice and usually involves the researcher observing an activity such as police–suspect interaction. The researcher plays no active role. For example, David J. Smith and Jeremy Grey went out on the beat with London Metropolitan police officers, while Aaron Victor Cicourel sat in the back of patrol cars and observed LA police officers interact with suspects and members of the general public.

2. Participant observation

This is the most common type of observation and involves sociologists immersing themselves in the lifestyle of the group they wish to study. Sociological observers participate in the same activities as the group being researched and observe their everyday lives.

Examiners' notes

Think about the strengths and weaknesses of using suicide notes to investigate motives for people killing themselves.

Essential notes

Both J. Maxwell Atkinson and Steve Taylor used this type of observation to observe coroners in action at inquests.

Examiners' notes

Make sure you are able to illustrate how this type of observation works in practice, with reference to particular studies.

This topic continues on the next two pages

The aim of participant observation is to understand what is happening from the point of view of those involved and to understand the meaning that they give to their situation. The research, then, is ethnographic – conducted in the natural environment of the group being studied. This type of research may take many months and even years to complete.

Participant observation can be either:

- Overt, when the researcher joins in the activities of a group but some or all of the group know his or her identity
  or
- Covert, when the researcher conceals the fact that she or he is doing research, and pretends to be a member of the group.

It can be very difficult to gain entry to a group, though some groups are easier to enter than others. For example, joining a football crowd is likely to be easier than joining a criminal gang.

A skilled researcher will focus on 'looking and listening', and going with the flow of social life, once he or she has gained entry to a group, and will not try to force the pace or interfere with or disrupt 'normality'. Instead, the skilled researcher will blend into the background until he or she has gained the group's trust and his or her presence is taken for granted. Much of participant observation, therefore, involves 'hanging around'.

Participant observation has a number of strengths and weaknesses.

Participant observation – strengths

- the researcher is placed in exactly the same situation as the group under study and large amounts of qualitative data are generated, giving the sociologist a feel for what it is like to be a member of the group
- what people say and what they actually do can be very different and people are often unaware that they are acting in a certain way (i.e. in observation studies, the sociologist can see what people really do and so is more likely to be able to record the truth, so validity is high)
- it can generate new ideas and lead to new insights (i.e. the sociologist might see things which inspire ideas that they would not have had if they had been using questionnaires and/or interviews)
- hypotheses can be changed or developed as the research progresses or as new situations are encountered, allowing an understanding of how changes in attitudes and behaviour take place over months and years

Participant observation – weaknesses

- presence of observer may result in the group acting less naturally because they are aware of being observed and studied, though covert observation is less likely to lead to this effect
- some observers can get too close or attached to 'their' group and consequently observations become biased (e.g. the observer may become overly sympathetic towards the group and 'go native', losing detachment and objectivity)

- no way of knowing if the researcher's findings are true or not since it is impossible to repeat the research and verify the data, so reliability is low
- the findings are merely the observer's view of things and he or she may use personal choice to select facts worth recording, which may match personal values and prejudices
- the sociologist must make value judgements in selecting what to include and what to omit from their final account, leaving a potential for bias because the sociologist may select aspects of the observation that fit his or her research hypothesis
- some sociologists object to this method because it lacks ethical consideration for those being researched especially if the research is covert. Laud Humphreys argues that some situations, particularly the study of deviant behaviour, will always have to involve some degree of deception to ensure validity. For example, it may involve the sociologist being forced to break the law in order to gain or retain the trust of the group, or to protect his or her cover. Humphreys therefore suggests that the situation determines the ethical approach – situational ethics.
- observation produces large amounts of qualitative data, which is difficult to analyse and categorize

Mixing methods

Triangulation involves the use of more than one research method or source of data in the course of a single study. A researcher can use more than one primary source and also use secondary data. Positivists promote the use of exclusively quantitative sources, whereas interpretivists prefer qualitative sources. In practice, many studies combine both types of sources and the triangulation of methods is common.

Types of triangulation

Martyn Hammersley (1996) distinguishes three ways of combining methods:

1. Triangulation – findings are cross-checked using a variety of methods; for example, interviews are used to check the responses made in questionnaires.
2. **Facilitation** – one method is used to assist or develop the use of another method; for example, in-depth unstructured interviews are used to devise questionnaire questions.
3. **Complementarity** – different methods are combined to dovetail different aspects of an investigation; for example, questionnaires might be used to discover overall statistical patterns and participant observation might be used to reveal the reasons for these patterns.

Essential notes

This observer effect can seriously undermine the validity of the research data. For example, the gang leader 'Doc' in William Whyte's research announced that he used to do things on instinct but now behaved differently because he felt he had to justify his actions to Whyte.

Essential notes

Paul Rock suggests that if the group a sociologist is observing no longer surprises or shocks the observer, the researcher has lost his or her objectivity and the research should end. Rock argues that a good observer should always be critical of the group they are studying.

Examiners' notes

Make sure you can identify at least three strengths and three weaknesses of covert participant observation compared to the more common overt version.

Examiners' notes

Triangulation may generate a small question in its own right but it is also useful for concluding discussions about any single method. To help you write conclusions in research method essays, use this section to point out that each method can be complemented with other methods, which provide different types of data or help to fill in the gaps.

Sociology and science

During the 19th century, the natural sciences proved successful in taking control of nature and producing technology that improved people's living standards. Positivist sociologists felt they could copy the success of science and produce a science of society, which could be used to eradicate problems such as poverty, injustice and conflict. Positivists believe that sociology is a science and that sociologists should seek to uncover the social laws that they believe underpin human behaviour by adopting the logic and methods of the natural sciences.

Positivist science is based on the **hypothetico-deductive model**, which stresses that scientific discovery should go through a number of logical stages:

Stage 1: An observation is made of social phenomena.

Stage 2: A hypothesis explaining the phenomena is formulated.

Stage 3: Evidence is collected in a systematic, objective and reliable fashion to deduce whether the hypothesis is true or false.

Stage 4: If sufficient data support the hypothesis, it becomes a theory and eventually a scientific or social law.

However, the positivist view of science and scientific method has been subjected to severe criticism over the years. Much of this critique has stemmed from the observation that positivist sociological research has not yet discovered any 'scientific' laws, despite a century of effort.

Karl Popper – philosopher of science

Philosophers of science such as Karl Popper have questioned the logic of the positivist hypothetico-deductive model because the emphasis in positivist research is on looking for evidence that confirms the hypothesis. Critics suggest that scientists should look for evidence that proves the hypothesis absolutely wrong and forces them to look elsewhere.

Popper claimed that there is no such thing as 'objective truth' that can be discovered and documented. At best, we can only achieve partial truth because all knowledge is provisional or temporary. This is because no matter how many times an experiment is conducted or a phenomenon is observed, the scientist can never be certain that the same results will be obtained in the future.

Popper illustrated this idea by using the hypothesis 'swans are always white'. He notes that many positivist scientists would be content to confirm this hypothesis after 999 observations of white swans. The notion that 'all swans are white' would become a scientific fact and it is unlikely that further observations would be conducted. However, Popper notes that this is bad science because there is always the possibility that a black swan will appear and prove this 'fact' wrong.

Popper argues that we can never be conclusively right, we can only be conclusively wrong. No amount of evidence in support of one hypothesis can ever prove that hypothesis right whereas a single piece of evidence that contradicts the hypothesis proves it absolutely wrong. Referring to his swan example, all the positivist scientist can say with any confidence is 'the swans observed so far are white'.

Popper argues that good science is about being rigorously sceptical and he proposed that scientific research methods should be based on the '**principle of falsification**', that is, instead of looking for evidence to prove a hypothesis right, scientists should look for evidence that proves it false. Popper argues that scientific knowledge is that which survives after rigorous testing – this knowledge can be tentatively accepted as close to the truth, although the possibility that one day contradictory evidence might appear denies it the status of real scientific truth.

Popper was sceptical about the scientific status of sociology because he argued that it was too theoretical and not engaged in enough testing or research. However, although this was probably true at the time Popper was writing, modern sociology has engaged extensively in the research process in ways that stress that nothing should ever be taken on trust and that evidence should be subjected to the most rigorous critical examination.

Evaluation of Karl Popper

Paul Feyerabend is critical of positivists and of Popper because both portray the scientific method as being a coldly logical and rational process. However, Feyerabend suggests that what scientists say they do is often different from what they actually do. He claims there is no such thing as a scientific method that is good for all times and in all places. Instead, he argues that in reality there is no logic to science – the rule seems to be 'anything goes'; individual scientists follow their own rules, which often do not resemble textbook models.

Abraham Kaplan agrees with Feyerabend and points out that many scientific discoveries are made almost by accident, and that inspired guesses, imagination, and luck play a crucial role in scientific research. Moreover, many scientists make false starts or collect data that takes them up blind alleys before they get back on track. Cheating is fairly common in science, mainly because scientists are heavily biased toward proving their own theories right. There is not much chance of being caught, as little attempt is made to replicate and verify the work of other scientists – there is no prestige in repeating someone else's work. Reliability in this sense is over-rated.

Scientific logic is imposed afterwards, during the writing-up process. Its function is to mystify scientific knowledge and to convince ordinary people that scientists deserve greater status and rewards because only scientists understand the logic of scientific enquiry.

This topic continues on the next two pages

Scientific Realism

Scientific Realists such as Andrew Sayer argue that many sciences theorize about the existence of phenomena which are difficult or impossible to observe, detect and therefore predict.

Examples of **open sciences** – concerned with the study of things we cannot see or sense directly – are seismology, meteorology, astronomy and some schools of physics such as cosmology. Sayer notes that open sciences are often unable to predict how the phenomena they are studying will behave. For example, seismologists cannot predict precisely when and where an earthquake will occur, so controlling variables is virtually impossible.

From a Realist position, sociology can be seen as scientific because it is largely concerned with developing models of underlying social structures and processes, which are largely unobservable but can be evaluated and modified by examining their effects. For example, social class as a social and economic force cannot be observed directly but its effects on social behaviour can be measured. So, in this sense, sociology could be classed as an open science.

Science and paradigms

Thomas Kuhn argues that scientists are not as open-minded as positivists claim. He rejects the idea that scientists are constantly making and testing hypotheses, arguing instead that they are concerned mainly with solving problems defined as important by earlier influential scientists. In other words, scientists usually work within a set of assumptions, left by an earlier generation of scientists, about what the natural world is like. Scientists take these assumptions as being correct, rather than questioning them. Kuhn calls these assumptions **paradigms** and argues that they shape and define scientists' views of the world – telling them what their priorities should be, what counts as legitimate evidence, how to approach specific problems and what scientific method to adopt.

Kuhn suggests that scientific progress only occurs because as time passes, more and more evidence, which does not fit the paradigm, appears. At first it is ignored or explained away, but eventually it becomes so numerous that the dominant paradigm loses credibility and is overthrown in a 'scientific revolution'. A new paradigm is established, and normal science resumes. Kuhn sees science as a body of knowledge constructed and created by scientists working within a specific paradigmatic context. So, scientific method is not free to wander as it wishes – it is constrained by accepted assumptions about how the world is organized.

Using Kuhn's definition of science, sociology is probably not scientific because it is doubtful if there has been one paradigm dominant at any one time within the discipline of sociology. Sociology has long been characterized by competing theoretical perspectives and even within these, there is intense disagreement.

Interpretivism and science

Interpretivist sociology is sceptical about positivist sociology's claim to scientific status and has generally taken an anti-positivist position.

Interpretivists do not believe sociology is scientific. They argue that the logic and methods of the natural sciences are unsuitable for sociology because its subject matter – humans – are active conscious beings, who are aware of what is going on around them and who constantly make choices about how to act and react.

Interpretivists reject the positivist notion that society is the product of social laws, so scientific procedures are needed to uncover these. Interpretivists argue that the focus of sociological research should be the interpretations or meanings that people bring to the social interactions that make up society.

Interpretivists argue for the adoption of research methods that help reveal the meanings that lie behind everyday social action. Mainly, they support the use of qualitative ethnographic methods, which focus on people in their everyday natural context and place emphasis upon *verstehen* (empathy with research subjects) and validity – the reality of those being studied. Positivist scientific methods are criticized and rejected by interpretivists, as, inevitably, they result in the sociologists' views of the world being imposed on the research subjects.

Postmodernism and science

Postmodernists reject the view that there exists any absolute and universal truth and knowledge. Therefore, they reject science as the embodiment of this idea. Postmodernists are especially critical of science because it claims to be objective. However, postmodernists argue that scientific knowledge is subjective and reflects the values of powerful Western interest groups. The rules of science such as logic and rationality are merely ways in which the powerful attempt to control ways of thinking.

Postmodernists argue that scientific truth and certainty are illusions constructed by Western academics. They argue that science has no more authority than other subjective versions of events. Postmodernists believe positivist sociology should abandon its search for ultimate truth because no such thing exists. They support a more pluralistic approach to scientific enquiry. They also prefer to use a range of research techniques to capture and analyse the many different interpretations of reality that postmodernists claim are found in postmodern society.

Essential notes

Some sociologists claim that sociology exists in a permanent state of revolution, whereas others claim sociology is in a pre-paradigmatic state, meaning that a single paradigm has yet to be accepted.

Essential notes

Interpretivist sociologists do not reject scientific principles altogether. They argue that reliability can still be achieved, but in different ways from those proposed by positivists. For example, observation data can be verified by checking and re-checking what has been observed and by supplementing observations with informal conversations with those being studied.

Examiners' notes

Exam questions on this topic usually focus on evaluating the idea that sociology can and should model itself on the natural sciences. Responses to this type of question should focus on how science is defined. Positivist definitions generally conflict with those of Popper, Kuhn and interpretivism.

Sociology and values

Value-free sociology

During the 19th century, Auguste Comte believed that sociology should be a **prescriptive** science of society. In his view, the purpose of sociology was to propose remedies for social and moral problems. This approach influenced the early poverty studies of Charles Booth and Seebohm Rowntree, which described the extent of poverty in the East End of London and York respectively and proposed remedies for its eradication.

However, in the early 20th century, positivist sociologists decided that it was not the sociologists' job to fix society. Instead, they argued, the role of sociology was to document social processes and problems in an objective way. It was the role of the social policy makers (such as politicians and civil servants) to act on sociological findings.

Positivists stressed 'objectivity through neutrality' – that sociologists should be the impartial and trustworthy pursuers of truth, so aiming only to see facts as they are – not as they might wish to see them. In this sense, sociologists aimed to be **value free** – not letting personal prejudices, tastes and beliefs influence their research methods or findings. They saw their job as simply to establish the truth about people's behaviour, not to praise or condemn it.

The idea that sociology should be value free became especially popular with functionalist sociologists in the USA, who in the post-war period were employed heavily by the state to advise the US army and large corporations.

The critique of value freedom

- Max Weber rejected the notion of value freedom. He argued that scientists and sociologists are also human, and citizens, and must not avoid the moral and political issues raised by their work by hiding behind words such as 'objectivity' or 'value freedom'. They must take moral responsibility for the harm their research might do.
- Alvin Gouldner agreed and argued that by the 1950s, American positivist sociologists had become 'spiritless technicians' who rarely questioned or criticized their paymasters.

Five broad criticisms of the concept of value freedom

1. Studies done by sociologists depend on those with power and funding, especially the government and large corporations, making value judgements about what is interesting and worthwhile. For example, corporate businesses have funded a huge amount of research in the USA aimed at improving worker productivity. Moreover, powerful groups have the power to resist sociological research. It is a fact that there have been many studies of the poor and the working class but relatively few studies of wealthy or powerful institutions such as public schools. Roger Gomm notes that value freedom often depends on who controls the values.
2. The personal values of sociologists may influence the choice of research topic, as they may wish to further their careers and reputations. Some sociologists censor themselves for fear that being

too outspoken will harm their career prospects or even cost them their job. Sociologists in university departments are also likely to be under pressure from universities to publish research, possibly regardless of its quality or usefulness.

3. Derek Phillips points out that data collection is itself a social process, so we can expect bias and invalidity to arise from the effects of interaction with research subjects. For example, in questionnaires and structured interviews, the sociologist has already decided which experiences of the subjects of research are important, by designing specific questions and providing a limited choice of response boxes to tick. By doing this, the sociologist imposes his or her values on the research subjects.

A major problem with interviews is the interview effect, in which interviewees may feel threatened by status differences between themselves and the interviewers. One effect is the **social desirability effect** – the interviewees work out the value position of the interviewers and provide the answers the interviewers are looking for – to please them.

Participant observation may result in the sociological observer **going native**. This means that he or she becomes too friendly with the people being observed, thus losing the ability to be objective and critical about the group's behaviour. Some observers, notably Sudhir Venkatesh, get so involved with a group that they engage in deviant behaviour.

There is a link between the kinds of methods sociologists prefer and their value stance. For example, interpretivists' preference for qualitative methods fits with their desire to empathize with the underdog, since such methods give them access to the actor's meanings and worldview (see pp 76–81). Functionalists tend to take the side of the 'establishment' and see things from the viewpoint of those in authority. This fits well with their uncritical acceptance of official government-produced statistics. Interactionists and functionalists can be accused of selecting methods that produce facts to reflect their values and outlook.

4. Alvin Gouldner argues that value-free sociology is a myth, as sociology is made up of socially organized knowledge, characterized by, for example, collective social values and prejudices. It is like this because sociologists are members of society and therefore cannot escape the influence of its culture and institutions. Gouldner argues that all researchers possess **domain assumptions** – a worldview which is the result of socialization into a certain culture. As a result, most American and European sociology reflects Western, capitalist and patriarchal values.

Gomm also notes that doing sociology is a social activity carried out by real people in a world characterized by conflicts of interest between different social groups. Therefore, any research must inevitably take one side or the other, whether the researcher admits this or not. Sociological research, according to Gomm, reflects ideological beliefs.

Essential notes

Not all sociologists will be influenced by who is paying their salaries. The Sociology Department of Leicester University was given £100 000 by the Conservative government in the 1980s to investigate football hooliganism. Leicester's findings based upon objective research were very critical of government policies aimed at solving this problem. In other words, they were not influenced by the fact that the government had paid for the research.

Essential notes

The findings of Sudhir Venkatesh in *Gang Leader For A Day* were partly shaped by the fact that he liked the people he was supposedly objectively observing.

Essential notes

Functionalist and New Right sociologists tend to stress that modern capitalist societies are characterized by order and consensus. Therefore, they very rarely engage in social dissent or criticism. They are much more likely to uncritically accept and support the way society is currently organized.

This topic continues on the next two pages

Essential notes

Some American sociologists, notably Walt Rostow, actually called communism a 'disease'.

Essential notes

Gomm implies that some groups are powerful enough to keep certain topics off the sociological research agenda. This may be one reason why many ordinary people are unaware of the great inequalities in income and wealth that characterize capitalist societies like the UK or are ignorant of ideas such as republicanism and humanism.

Essential notes

Gouldner criticizes Becker for taking a romantic and sentimental approach to disadvantaged groups.

For example, functionalist sociologists believe that society is characterized by a consensus on values. Such sociologists tend not to engage in social criticism of the way capitalist societies are organized – instead they support the status quo and thus establishment values. Such sociologists are likely to believe that poverty is the fault of the individual, or working-class culture, or the welfare state, rather than the way capitalism is organized. They are more interested in working-class crime than white-collar or corporate crime. Functionalist sociologists, such as Talcott Parsons, have been accused of being patriarchal because they believe in distinct gender roles within the family and that only the male should perform the breadwinner role and only the female should perform the nurturing role.

5. Gomm suggests that by presenting facts as 'truth', sociologists are able to deny responsibility for the way in which their research is used by policy makers. For example, **compensatory education** was introduced into UK schools in the 1960s because sociologists convinced politicians that working-class culture was inferior and required a helping hand in the form of extra resources. However, Gomm points out that this policy distracted from other possible causes of working-class educational underachievement such as the role of schools and teachers, or the economic advantages enjoyed by the middle classes, or private schooling. Gomm suggests that the most important aspect of sociological research is what is *not* investigated.

For example, a sociological study of homelessness may investigate the social background of the homeless but may ignore the workings of the property market, which may be responsible for the housing shortage. Such a study will lead only to politically safe conclusions that blame the victims. Gomm suggests that such sociological research is ideological because it helps to maintain inequality.

Critical politicized sociology

Some sociologists have rejected the concept of value freedom, suggesting that it is undesirable to pretend to be value free. For example, many Marxists feel they should side with the working class and feminists side with women, while many interactionist studies side with the 'deviant'.

Howard Becker argues that sociologists should adopt a compassionate stance and side with the underdogs – criminals, mental patients and other powerless groups – because less is known about these groups and their stories should be told in order to redress the balance of power in society. As a result, interactionists have a strong preference for qualitative methods such as participant observation, which they see as revealing how the 'outsiders' view and interpret the social world.

All these critical perspectives acknowledge that values do and should enter sociological research. Sociologists argue that sociology should not and cannot be morally neutral or indifferent. Instead, it should be **value laden**. Moreover, sociology should be politically prescriptive and suggest ways forward in order to create a better society.

Such ideas do not necessarily mean that the research will be biased and therefore unreliable and invalid. Good sociology still rests on the ability of sociologists to demonstrate the truth of their ideas empirically rather than merely by being committed to certain value positions. Effective sociology still needs to be committed to concepts such as reliability, validity and representativeness.

However, postmodernism rejects the idea that any one sociological account of the social world is superior to another. Any perspective that claims to have the truth, such as Marxism, functionalism or feminism, is just a meta-narrative or 'big story'. All knowledge, from any perspective, is based on values and assumptions. Thus, no perspective has any special claim to be true. However postmodernism has been criticized for being logically self-defeating, since it claims to be telling us something true, while simultaneously telling us that no one can tell us what is true.

Essential notes

Sociologists are like doctors and scientists, who may also be motivated by a sense of social justice and emotional commitment to the health of their patients, but this does not mean that they are prevented from conducting an objective investigation into the causes of ill health.

Examiners' notes

Note that in some 33-mark Theory and Method exam questions, the focus may be on whether values can and should be kept out of sociological research.

Sociology and social policy

In order to understand the role of sociology in relation to social policy, it is useful to distinguish between social and sociological problems. Peter Worsley defines a 'social problem' as 'some piece of social behaviour that causes public friction and/or private misery'. For example, poverty, juvenile delinquency and divorce may all be regarded as social problems by members of society, and governments may be called upon to produce policies to tackle the problems.

According to Worsley, a sociological problem is any pattern of social relationships or behaviour. This might be something that society regards as a social problem or behaviour that society does not normally regard as a problem, for example, why people conform or are committed to school or work. In other words, 'normal' behaviour is just as interesting to sociologists as behaviour that people see as a social problem.

The influence of sociology on policy

However, even when sociologists do conduct research into social problems, there is no guarantee that policy makers will use their findings, or that any solutions they propose will find their way into social policies. Many factors affect whether or not sociological research succeeds in influencing government policy, including:

- Electoral popularity – research findings might produce a policy that would be unpopular with voters.
- Ideological and policy preferences of governments – if the researcher's value stance is similar to the political ideology of the government, the value stance may stand more chance of influencing its policies.
- Interest groups – pressure groups that seek to influence government policies in their own interests; these groups may be powerful enough to persuade the government to ignore sociological research findings.
- Globalization – social policy is increasingly influenced by global interests such as the European Union (EU) and the International Monetary Fund (IMF).
- Critical sociology – sociologists such as Marxists, who are critical of the capitalist state and large corporations, are often ignored by social policy makers.
- Cost – even if the government is sympathetic to the sociologist's findings, it may have other spending priorities and commitments.
- Funding sources – in some cases, sociologists may tone down their findings and policy recommendations because they want to continue to do research in the future and do not want to risk alienating their paymasters.

Perspectives on social policy and sociology

Different sociological perspectives hold different views of the nature of the state and the social policy it produces.

Functionalists see the state as serving the interests of society as a whole, to produce and implement rational social policies for the good of all. The sociologist's role is to provide the state with the objective, scientific information needed to implement social policy effectively. Functionalists usually favour cautious 'piecemeal social engineering', which tackles only one issue at a time.

The **social democratic perspective** is more radical and favours a major redistribution of wealth and income from the rich to the poor. Peter Townsend argues that sociologists should be involved in researching social problems such as poverty and should make specific policy recommendations so that social policy can aim to eradicate them.

Marxists see the state in capitalist societies as an instrument of the ruling class and its social policies as serving the interests of capitalism rather than the interests of society as a whole. For example, the welfare state exists in order to make it appear as though capitalists care about the poor, the sick and the old. However, the real purpose of the welfare state is to maintain the health and welfare of the working class so that they can be exploited to full effect at work, and to buy off working-class opposition to capitalism. Marxists argue that the only solution to social problems is to overthrow capitalism and create an alternative classless society. The sociologist's job is to reveal to the working class the exploitation and inequality that underpin capitalism so that Marxists can act to do this.

Feminists see society as patriarchal, and the state as a patriarchal institution, which perpetuates women's subordination through its social policies. For example, family policies often assume that women should be mostly responsible for nurturing children. However, **liberal feminists** believe that social policy in the form of anti-discrimination reforms will ultimately bring about gender equality. The **radical feminist** critique of male violence has led to positive social policy of domestic violence.

The New Right believe that the state should have minimal involvement in society. They are opposed to using state provision of welfare to deal with social problems. In their view, state intervention in areas such as welfare robs people of their freedom to make their own choices and undermines their sense of responsibility. This, in turn, leads to greater social problems such as crime and delinquency. The New Right also support a strong 'law and order' policy, and research by Right Realist criminologists has been influential in the widespread introduction of zero tolerance crime policies.

Essential notes

Marxists claim that both the functionalist and social democratic approaches fail to deal with the real cause of inequality, which is the way capitalism is organized.

Essential notes

Critics argue that Marxist views on social policy and the role of sociologists are impractical and unrealistic.

Essential notes

Feminist sociological research has had some impact on social policies in areas that affect women, in part due to the success of the broader feminist movement in gaining greater political influence since the 1970s.

Essential notes

New Right thinking has been very influential on Labour and Conservative governments with regard to family and crime policies.

Examiners' notes

Theory and Method exam questions for 33 marks usually focus quite straightforwardly on the relationship between sociology and social policy.

General tips for the Crime and Deviance exam

The Unit 4 Crime and Deviance examination paper consists of four compulsory questions, to be completed in two hours. The maximum mark for this paper is 90, so this is under one and a half minutes per mark, once you have taken off time for reading. Remember to allocate your time according to the number of marks in each question.

For each question, more marks are awarded for AO2 skills than for AO1 skills. At A2 level, you are expected to show that you can interpret questions well and then apply relevant material to answer the question. You should also show good analysis and evaluation skills – you need to unpack and discuss issues, not just describe theories and research. You will also show these skills by having a clear focus on the question set, rather than writing in general about the topic area. You will be given three Items to help you with some of the questions. Once you are familiar with the questions, read the Items carefully to identify points or issues you can use. Bear in mind that the Items only provide you with a starting point; this is **not** a comprehension.

- **Questions 01** and **02** are essay questions worth 21 marks each. Each question will ask you to use an Item. Bear in mind that if you do not do so, you will not gain top marks. Try to build on the Item by developing some of the ideas. Remember that 'and elsewhere' means that you are expected to contribute many of your own ideas – the Item will not provide everything you need. The questions will usually ask you to 'assess', which involves evaluation and judgement. Of the marks for this essay, 12 are for AO2 skills and only 9 marks are for AO1 skills. Make sure you include references to the wording of the question, to sociological concepts and perspectives, and that you cover all the elements in the question. Start with a short introduction of the most important elements of the question and end with a brief conclusion, bringing all the main themes of your essay together.
- **Question 03** is the Methods in Context question. This is a similar format to the Methods in Context question on Unit 2. However, you are given less direct help here than at AS level, but will be expected to focus more clearly on the issue. Do not spend time talking about sociological views on the issue. Instead, focus on the method. You should show that you understand the strengths and weaknesses of the method in question, but good application of these to investigating the specific issue is what will gain you high marks. You should consider the research characteristics of the group and/ or situation and then consider how these facts affect the way the method can be applied and how successful it might be. The more you can apply the strengths and weaknesses of the method to the specific group, situation and issue, the more marks you will gain.
- **Question 04** is the essay question on Theory and Methods. It is 'free-standing' – it will not have an Item to refer to. This question is worth 33 marks: 15 for AO1 skills; 9 for interpretation and application; 9 for analysis and evaluation. As with questions 01 and 02, you will be asked to 'assess'. Make sure you focus clearly on the question set. Remember that this section is Theory and Methods – if the question seems to focus on methods of research, make sure you link

the issues clearly to theoretical perspectives such as positivist and interpretivist approaches, and always discuss theoretical issues as well as practical ones.

When writing each essay, you should look back regularly to the question. Make sure you have obeyed all the instructions and covered all the issues included in the question. Some essays have two or more parts. You will not gain top marks if you do not address each part. It's also very important to focus on the question set. Do not be tempted to write an essay about all you know on a topic in a question, or to spend time writing at a tangent to the question – use your material to focus on the issues.

Note for 2011 candidates

The format for the examination described here will be used from January 2012 onwards.

- In June 2011, the essay questions 01 and 02 will still be following the old format. Questions 01 and 02 will be worth 12 marks and 21 marks, not 21 marks each, as shown here. This means that question 01 will require less from candidates in terms of both breadth and depth.
- However, in June 2011 there will be an additional question, worth 9 marks, on Methods in Context. This question is likely to ask you about using particular methods in particular circumstances. For example, you could be asked to explain two or three problems and/or advantages of using, say, self-report studies, official statistics or participant observation when investigating a particular deviant group. Alternatively, you could split this question into two parts, to ask about one advantage and two problems, for example.

Crime and Deviance (sample exam paper 1)

Read Items 1A, 1B and 1C below, and answer the questions that follow.

Item 1A

According to official crime statistics, 80% of convicted offenders in England and Wales are male, although self-report studies suggest that the real difference between male and female crime rates may not actually be so great. Females also commit different kinds of crimes to males. For example, typical female crimes are shoplifting or property crime, whereas males are far more likely than females to be convicted of violent or drug offences.

More females than males are victims of crimes such as sexual assault, but these crimes are under-reported and therefore less likely to be prosecuted. In addition, according to Stewart (2006), perceptions of female offenders in court are significantly influenced by conventional stereotypes of gender roles as wives and mothers. Those who do not conform to such stereotypes may be punished more severely.

Item 1B

Realist approaches see crime as a real problem to be dealt with, not just a social construction. Both Left and Right Realists therefore criticize those who focus only on the criminal justice system and the reporting and recording of crime. Realists take crime rates seriously.

However, there are important differences. Right Realists, such as Murray, see crime as the result of the choices made by individuals, whereas Left Realists such as Young argue that crime is caused by structural factors. As a result, Left and Right Realists disagree on how to reduce crime.

Item 1C

Investigating young offenders and violent crime

It is very unlikely that a researcher would have the opportunity to witness violent crime as it happens. This type of crime often takes place quickly, in a secluded area, with little advance notice. Any researcher arriving on the scene is likely to be ushered away by the police for his or her own safety. This means that investigations must take place later, relying on memory and cooperation from those involved.

Young offenders are likely to be under-achievers and belong to anti-authority subcultures. These characteristics have implications for the way research is conducted. On the one hand these offenders may be vulnerable, as possible victims, as well as offenders. Conversely, they may be more prepared to use violence than other respondents.

The use of written questionnaires enables the researcher to avoid possible danger and any ethical issues that might arise. It also means that there is the potential to collect a wide range of data.

Questions

01 Using material from **Item 1A** and elsewhere, assess sociological explanations of female patterns of offending, victimization and punishment. **[21 marks]**

02 Using material from **Item 1B** and elsewhere, assess the contribution of Realist approaches to our understanding of crime. **[21 marks]**

03 Using material from **Item 1C** and elsewhere, assess the strengths and limitations of written questionnaires as a means of investigating young offenders and violent crime. **[15 marks]**
*This question requires you to **apply** your knowledge and understanding of sociological research methods to the study of this **particular** issue in **crime and deviance.***

04 Assess the contribution of interactionist theory and research to our understanding of society. **[33 marks]**

Grade A answer

01 *Using material from **Item 1A** and elsewhere, assess sociological explanations of female patterns of offending, victimization and punishment.* [**21 marks**]

A good introduction, showing knowledge of the extent and types of female offending, plus a reference to women as victims. There is no mention of punishment, however.

Official statistics would suggest that females are far less likely to commit crime than men, with only 20% of convictions being for women in 2006. Within this, the most common age of female conviction is for 16-year-old offenders. Statistics also show that 50% of crimes committed by women are theft and handling stolen goods, compared to only 30% of males. The British Crime Survey (BCS) shows that women are also at a much higher risk to victimization of violent domestic crime and sexual offences than are males.

A brief but appropriate account of sex role theory.

The first sociological explanations for low rates of female crime concentrated on functionalist ideas of female sex roles and socialization. This was based on Parson's idea of women taking the 'expressive' role in the family. Girls are brought up to follow their mothers as role models. As they are taught to be caring and nurturing, this prevents women from engaging in crime, in contrast to the males, who are encouraged to be competitive and strong. This may also mean that men are more violent and may learn more technical skills that could be useful for crime.

This paragraph provides a good account of feminist theories of opportunity and control, with some appropriate analysis. Another useful source would be Carlen's work on gender and class deals.

However, feminists see the pattern of low female offending as the product of a patriarchal society in which men control women, through violence if necessary. Thus women don't get as much chance to commit crime, as they are so controlled. They are expected to look after the children and take care of the home, on top of having a career, which leaves little time for deviance. On the other hand, men are socialized into a hegemonic masculinity that accepts violence and aggression as normal. Also, this dominant form of masculinity may place a high value on thrill-seeking and risk-taking and these may lead to deviant acts, as sociologists such as Lyng point out. For women, their crimes often reflect their traditional female role – such as shoplifting. Heidensohn identifies two other ways in which women are controlled. As well as in the home, women are controlled in public places by abuse from boys and the fear of being attacked or losing their good reputation. This happens at work too – women are often in inferior positions and may suffer sexual harassment. Overall, this means that women have far fewer opportunities for crime.

The focus here moves to a consideration of punishment, with a good explanation of the chivalry thesis.

In terms of punishment, we must consider the 'chivalry thesis'. This is the suggestion that the police and courts treat women more kindly, so they are less likely to be arrested, charged and found guilty. This is because most of these positions are filled by men, who still tend to hold to the traditional views of women as being gentle and caring – so are less likely to see them as criminals. They are more likely to give women a warning or caution, rather than arrest and prosecute them. Therefore, this suggests that the statistics are inaccurate, as they don't take into account many crimes that are actually committed by women. This ties in with statistics from self-report studies that show much higher figures for female crime than the official ones. ☞

However, Heidensohn suggests that sometimes women are treated worse. They are more likely to be convicted if they appear to be deviating from the socially accepted models of sexuality and Carlen argues that convictions are based more on the female's ability as a wife, mother or daughter than the actual crime itself. She found Scottish judges were less likely to jail women they saw as good mothers. As Item 1A says, 'those who do not conform to such stereotypes may be punished more severely'. Some women offenders may be seen as 'doubly deviant' – deviant in the sense of committing crime but also deviant in the sense of not conforming to traditional feminine norms and values. Girls are often punished by the courts for promiscuous behaviour, and are far more likely to be put into care 'for their own good', even when they have not committed a crime.

An alternative view, linked to the Item, is well explained and sourced.

Buckle and Farrington also provide evidence against the chivalry thesis. They found that women were not given lower sentences for the same offences. Box suggests that it's simply that women commit lesser offences anyway – when they commit really serious crimes they are treated the same.

Two further brief points of evaluation.

Women may also be victimized. Feminists in particular point to the domestic violence and sexual abuse experienced by women, only a small amount of which is reported and recorded. Radical feminists see this violence as a crucial way in which men control women and so reproduce patriarchy. Often research suggests women are attacked when seen as not playing their stereotyped role properly, for example, when dinner is late.

The third aspect, of victimization, is tackled, though this is rather thin.

In recent years there has been an increase in female crime rates anyway. Most sociologists see this as the result of women's liberation and the increased numbers at work – so having more opportunities. In particular, more career women in high level jobs will mean more chance of white-collar crime. There has also been a rise in girl gangs in big cities, where some working-class girls follow the same pattern as boy gangs.

A good paragraph, challenging the material previously mentioned via the liberation thesis. This could be used more effectively, with explicit reference to the thesis and its critics.

The patterns in Item 1A show that women are convicted of less crime than men, but levels of actual crimes committed might not be as unequal as statistics show. It is more that women are judged on their capabilities as a stereotypical woman. They are more likely to be a victim of violent and sexual crimes than men are in the home. However, men are more likely to be attacked by a stranger. Feminists argue that the crime and justice systems are very biased when it comes to women, and higher levels of equality need to be reached.

The conclusion provides a good summary plus another evaluative point.

Overall this is a good essay. The question asks for a broad range to be covered, as there are three different aspects to deal with. This answer includes all three, though there is less coverage of victimization. However, there does not have to be equal balance to gain high marks. The focus is on females throughout; the temptation to explain patterns of male crime is resisted. Several different sociological explanations are outlined and a good range of concepts and sources are used. Several points from the Item are taken up but some links could be made more explicitly. The skills of analysis and evaluation are shown in a number of places.
Mark 18/21

02 *Using material from **Item 1B** and elsewhere, assess the contribution of Realist approaches to our understanding of crime.* **[21 marks]**

A very good introduction, putting Realist theories into context.

As stated in Item 1B, 'Realists take crime rates seriously', they see crime as a real indicator of a real social problem. Realist approaches appeared in the 1980s and attempted to look at crime in a more practical way than some previous sociological explanations such as Marxism and labelling theory. Realist approaches accepted official statistics of crime and recognized the damage crime did to victims' lives. They focused their attention on making practical suggestions to reduce and combat crime. Realist approaches differ in their political viewpoints. Right Realists are more linked to conservative views and Left Realists are linked to socialist political views.

This is a rather limited explanation of Right Realist theory, focusing only on socialization and omitting important aspects such as rational choice theory and biosocial theory.

Right Realists argues that the cause of crime can be found in the 'underclass'. Charles Murray argues that this represents a breakdown of moral values and traditions, through births outside marriage and single-parent families headed by females. Murray argues that these lead to inadequate socialization and a lack of a male role model leads to an increase in crime.

A good paragraph, focusing on the possible solutions presented by Right Realism. A hint of evaluation is present but not developed.

Another Right Realist, Wilson would say that once crime is allowed to happen on a small scale, it will happen on a big scale. For example, a youth who starts vandalizing property and commits other minor offences will go on to perform much larger crimes such as GBH and robbery, if they are not stopped fairly quickly. This is the 'broken windows' theory – if one broken window is left, the rest will be broken. Wilson says that therefore it is the responsibility of the local community to make sure that petty crime is disapproved of, and of the police to concentrate on changing people's views of what is socially acceptable. This should cut crime off at the source and thus severely decrease the levels of 'big' crimes that happen. Although this theory can be criticized for concentrating predominantly on working-class crime and ignoring the powerful, it gives another explanation for crime. This theory provoked the idea of 'zero tolerance' policing, to crack down immediately on any minor disorder such as rowdiness. This was enforced originally in New York, then in other parts of America and England, and led to a noticeable decrease in crime rates.

A good range of concepts are used here to explain further Right Realist policies. Some good evaluation is included.

Right Realists also argue that to prevent crime communities need to be more integrated using informal controls, and have increased surveillance and target hardening. Increasing surveillance includes more CCTVs at shops, and more stops and searches. Individuals and companies are encouraged to take greater precautions against crime with more car alarms, fences and security guards. Overall this means it's harder to commit crimes and easier to get caught. However, this 'situational crime prevention' is criticized because it doesn't reduce crime, it simply displaces it to somewhere else. Delinquents would move to poorer areas with less security, where crime becomes concentrated. This has been referred to as 'urban apartheid' because the rich are in gated communities with high security and the poor are in crime-ridden ghettos. ☞

According to Left Realists Lea and Young, this increases the feelings of marginalization for the young in these areas, which is likely to lead to more crime. Left Realists argue that there are several explanations for why the poor commit crime. These are relative deprivation, marginalization and subcultures. Left Realists, such as Young, don't see crime so much as down to the individual, but more a result of structural factors such as inequality leading to feelings of relative deprivation. This means that people turn to crime when they compare themselves to others who are a lot better off. The media exposes them to glamorous consumer goods but they are excluded from these. This leads to feelings of marginalization and failure – being on the edge of society, rather than in the mainstream, both economically and socially. For example, young people in council housing suffer from marginalization because they will be on a low income and have very little influence over decisions made on their behalf. Those who have been marginalized may feel they don't belong to the larger society, so this leads to the formation of deviant subcultures, as this can give them their own status and values, opposed to the mainstream.

Left Realists also focus on policing and they argue that it should be geared to the public's needs. They say that the police must involve the public more, as they are dependent on the public for information on 90% of crimes. They need to consult the public and focus on the things the public see as important. If they use military policing styles they will alienate the public's support.

Overall both Left and Right Realist approaches have been influential in dealing with crime and could be the reason why crime rates have been falling. An example of this is Tony Blair's 'Tough on crime, tough on the causes of crime', which used bits of both theories. Unlike most theories, they both look at possible solutions.

A good link is made to a contrast with Left Realism and an explanation of its main theoretical concepts.

A limited account of solutions put forward by Left Realists.

The conclusion makes a valid link between Realism and policy in action. Both this and the final brief evaluative point could be analysed more effectively.

Overall this is a good answer. For Right Realism, there is good analysis of the possible solutions put forward but their explanations for crime are dealt with rather superficially. For Left Realism, the picture is reversed, in that the theory is explained well but the possible solutions are dealt with in a more cursory fashion. There is good evidence of all skills, however, and a good range of sociological concepts and sources are used. It would be useful to show clearly how these theories differ from previous sociological perspectives on crime.

Mark 16/21

03 *Using material from* **Item 1C** *and elsewhere, assess the strengths and limitations of written questionnaires as a means of investigating young offenders and violent crime.* [**15 marks**]

This opening paragraph lists a range of strengths and weaknesses of written questionnaires in general. These points are valid but not specific to the situation in the question.

Questionnaires are notoriously low in validity, as participants have to pick from a choice of answers that don't always reflect their exact feelings. However, they are high in reliability, as the questions are the same whenever they are used. Also, they are fairly easy to analyse, so large numbers of them can be taken, which means there is a large range of data. Questionnaires are often a quick and cheap way to gain information.

Good application. Another potential strength and two potential weaknesses are outlined – the issues of language and understanding are applied successfully to the issue in the question.

Regarding youth offenders and violent crimes, questionnaires may be a good way of getting data, as they can be easy to complete. However, this may be a problem – as Item 1C says, this particular group of offenders are likely to be low achievers, so the language used, the complexity of the questions and the length of the questionnaire might all be problems. They may use their own slang in their answers, which could also mean the researcher doesn't fully understand the answers. If the language is complex then the offenders may not understand the questions as they may have low levels of literacy, and an interview would have been more appropriate.

Again, the problem of group awareness is applied to the specific issue.

Written questionnaires are often given out and then returned later, which sometimes causes a problem of validity. In this case, the young people may answer them together. They may well be members of a close-knit delinquent subculture – if they answer them together, the answers will not be as valid as individual views.

Good paragraph. The problem of low response rates is successfully applied to the issue and some analysis provided.

Low response rates are often cited as a big problem with questionnaires, which could lead to serious validity problems with this method. If young offenders have trouble understanding the questionnaires, they are unlikely to return them. Young offenders are likely to be suspicious of authority and may associate the questionnaire with incriminating themselves. They might lie in their answers or exaggerate their crimes in order to achieve status within their subculture. They might also underestimate their experiences of victimization and not wish to admit these, as they are 'vulnerable as possible victims as well as offenders'.

Good focus on the issue of danger. Written questionnaires are contrasted with other possible methods.

One advantage in using written questionnaires when studying violent crime is that there is probably less danger than with other methods because the researcher doesn't need to get close to the gang or 'fit in'. Researchers will not need to be trained or change the way they behave or dress in order to hand out questionnaires. So there is probably less threat of violence than with interviews or participant observation.

Perhaps a bit of an afterthought, but another valid issue is raised. However, this is related to the use of questionnaires in general when studying crime, not to the specific issue in the question.

Finally, there may still be ethical issues with questionnaires. What if a respondent admits to more serious crimes on the questionnaire? To what extent should they be allowed to be anonymous?

Overall, this is a sound answer with good focus on the issue of using written questionnaires to investigate young offenders and violent crime. A range of strengths and limitations of the method are included, though these tend to be listed rather than developed in the first paragraph. However, the answer then focuses well on more strengths and weaknesses, while considering these with regard to the study of young offenders and the study of violent crime. A good range of research characteristics for both young offenders and violent crime are included.

Other relevant issues might include: the possible problems of carrying out such work in a high-crime area; young offenders may be under-age and vulnerable (but also violent), therefore parental consent might be required for ethical reasons – but would parents be happy for their children to answer such questions? In addition, the method relies on memory, which could be confused.

Mark: 13/15

---

04 *Assess the contribution of interactionist theory and research to our understanding of society.* **[33 marks]**

Interactionism is an 'action' approach. Whereas structural theories such as functionalism and Marxism focus on the way in which the structure of society determines how individuals act, interactionists are less interested in the 'big picture' of society and more interested in the small-scale interactions between individuals. They want to understand how people are influenced by one another and their own perceptions of the social world.

Interactionists see people as having free will to make their own choices as to what they do. They have been very influential in the study of the meanings people attach to their behaviour rather than just the behaviour itself. For example, Mead explained how we use symbols in our interaction that must be interpreted by another person. In order to do this, according to Mead, we must 'take the role of the other' and see our own behaviour through their eyes. We have to learn to do this as children by taking on different roles through play. Similarly, Blumer used Mead's ideas to establish his three principles of human behaviour – that actions are based on meanings; that meanings are not fixed but arise from interaction; and that these meanings are determined by how we interpret actions. These theories are very different from the 'top-down' theories of earlier sociology and therefore contribute useful insights into behaviour that structural theories do not.

One approach based on interactionism is the development of labelling theory. This idea is that deviance is not 'real' but in fact a 'label' that some people attach to other people's actions. Once 'labelled', people may change their behaviour and actually become deviant – known as a self-fulfilling prophecy. Cooley said this was because we develop a 'looking-glass self'. We develop a self-concept by taking the role of the other and seeing ourselves as ☞

A good introductory paragraph, explaining the meaning of interactionism.

Several points about interactionism are explained and developed through the work of Mead and Blumer. A number of useful concepts are included. A clear reference is made to the question, showing the particular contribution of interactionism.

One interactionist approach and several concepts are outlined and examples are provided. Two evaluative points are made.

others see us. So there is a self-fulfilling prophecy and we become what others see us as. Howard Becker, who coined the term 'labelling', showed how a student might achieve less because of accepting the view of him or her, held by a teacher, and so it became a self-fulfilling prophecy. Once labelled, a person might develop a 'deviant career' and live out the label more and more. Cohen also showed how the media can cause secondary deviance in his research on the creation of moral panics. Labelling theory shows how labelling affects whole groups, for example, Hall shows how young black males are often labelled as 'muggers' and this can affect the way the police deal with them, making the situation worse and actually encouraging deviant behaviour. This approach questions the structuralist assumption that deviance is produced by factors such as poor socialization or deprivation. However, this idea of labelling in some ways seems to contradict earlier interactionists, as labelling is criticized for being too deterministic – meaning that the person being labelled has no free choice. People may actually choose to be deviant.

A further approach is outlined and explained.

Another interactionist approach is Goffman's dramaturgical model. He focuses on how people shape their own selves by influencing other people's impressions of them. Like actors, people play roles and present an impression of themselves to others. Goffman calls this 'impression management' – the way we use all sorts of techniques such as language and dress to make sure others see us as we want them to see us. And we check their responses to see if we need to change anything in the way we behave to make our 'act' more convincing.

A good, evaluative paragraph. Interactionism is contrasted with structuralist views and several critical points are raised. The point from Becker adds more analytical depth, but the final point is rather weak.

Interactionism has been criticized by other perspectives for being too limited in scope. It doesn't take into account the wider social structure or where the meanings come from in the first place. Why are members of a particular social class or ethnic group labelled much more than others? Where do the police get their labels? It is also said to ignore the importance of power. Marxists believe it focuses on trivial aspects of society and ignores 'the big picture' of the social structure, social inequality and exploitation of the proletariat by the bourgeoisie. By focusing on labelling, interactionism ends up criticizing teachers and the police rather than the really powerful upper class – the people who make the rules in the first place. However, Becker does point out that some groups, like teachers and the police, are more powerful than others and are therefore more able to do the labelling. So, it may be possible to combine some of the features of both approaches.

Two more brief but valid criticisms are made here.

Another criticism of labelling theory is that it assumes that deviance is caused by labelling and without it deviance would not exist. But certain acts are deviant or illegal and are never discovered. Also, many criminals know they are committing crimes, without someone labelling them.

The analysis of interactionism is extended to include some aspects of methodology. Two more examples of research are provided.

To investigate the processes of, for example, labelling, interactionists have often used interpretive research methods, such as participant observation, rather than quantitative positivist methods. This approach to research, when the sociologist actually joins in with the group they are studying, enables the researcher to empathize with the group and achieve what Weber called *verstehen* – empathetic understanding. This enables the researcher to see ☞

how the group makes sense of the situation and can produce in-depth explanations of behaviour. For example, Venkatesh's study of gangs in Chicago (based on participant observation) took place over several years and allowed him to find out exactly why members of the gang behaved in the way they did. Barker used participant observation in her study of the Moonies, which enabled her to find out that their constant attempts to sell their religion on the streets were in fact a way of convincing themselves of their beliefs.

However, this method of participant observation is also criticized for being impossible to replicate and therefore completely unreliable. It is also biased, as the researcher usually ends up sympathizing and siding with the group they are studying rather than keeping an objective view.

Two brief evaluative comments on the research method.

In conclusion, interactionism has given sociologists many insights into the way people's interaction affects the way society works and has provided a range of richly detailed research. It has introduced the ideas of labelling and symbolic interaction, but perhaps it needs to be mixed with a more structural approach to provide a full picture of society.

The first sentence in this conclusion refers back very successfully to the question – to contribution, to theory and to research.

Overall, this is a good answer. A good range of examples of interactionist theories and concepts are provided, and a number of criticisms are suggested. Explanations of these are good but could have more breadth. There is good evidence of analysis and evaluation. The answer deals with both theory and research and tries in several places to answer the question of the contribution of interactionism to our understanding of society.
Mark: 12/15 + 7/9 + 6/9 = 25/33

Total marks: 18 + 16 + 13 + 25 = 72/90 = Grade A

Crime and Deviance (sample exam paper 2)

Read Items 2A, 2B and 2C below, and answer the questions that follow.

Item 2A

In 2008, according to Home Office statistics, Asians were twice as likely, and Blacks seven times more likely, to be stopped and searched than Whites. Blacks were five times, and Asians one and a half times more likely than Whites to be in the prison population, compared to their proportion in the general population.

Some sociologists suggest that this is because some ethnic groups suffer deprivation and are therefore more likely to offend than others. However, others argue that the differences in crime rates are the result of racism within the criminal justice system.

Item 2B

Functionalist sociologists portray society as stable and conforming, with a system of norms and values on which there is consensus. This is the basis of social order in society.

However, deviance entails the breaking of social norms and so must be seen as a threat to the stability of society. Durkheim deals with this issue by arguing that some deviance may be functional for society and even inevitable in all societies. Later functionalists have suggested a number of structural and cultural reasons to explain deviance in society. For example, strain theory shows how the same structural factors that encourage success for many individuals, can lead to deviance by others.

Item 2C

Investigating the relationship between media use and fear of crime

Studies have revealed that the fear of crime is widespread. Up to one-third of the inhabitants in some areas feel unsafe even in their own homes, and many people may alter their behaviour to avoid the possibility of becoming a victim. This is particularly true of women.

The media frequently focus on crime. They are accused of exaggerating crime in general and violent sexual crime especially, as such subjects are seen as being newsworthy. Young women and old people are often seen as likely victims. Because of this exaggeration, many sociologists argue that the media produce a level of fear that is unrealistic. Schlesinger and Tumber (1992) found that those who watched a lot of television and read tabloid newspapers were more likely to have strong fears.

Structured interviews can provide a representative picture of fear of crime, as they can be used with a wide range of people but also allow some personal contact.

Questions

01 Using material from **Item 2A** and elsewhere, assess the usefulness of conflict theories in understanding ethnic differences in crime rates.
[**21 marks**]

02 'Consensus theories such as functionalism provide the most useful analysis of the causes of deviance in society'
Assess this view, using material from **Item 2B** and elsewhere.
[**21 marks**]

03 Using material from **Item 2C** and elsewhere, assess the strengths and limitations of structured interviews as a means of investigating the relationship between media use and fear of crime. [**15 marks**]
This question requires you to **apply** *your knowledge and understanding of sociological research methods to the study of this* **particular** *issue in* **crime and deviance.**

04 Evaluate different views of the relationship between sociology and social policy. [**33 marks**]

Grade C answer

01 *Using material from **Item 2A** and elsewhere, assess the usefulness of conflict theories in understanding ethnic differences in crime rates.*
[21 marks]

A reasonable introduction, outlining some theoretical positions, though this is rather narrow in focus.

Conflict theories view society as an unequal system that brings about conflict. This includes Marxism, which argues that crime is generated from today's capitalist society. Marxist sociologists believe that selective law enforcement against the working class serves to maintain ruling class power and reinforce ruling class ideology. Neo-Marxist theories also exist – these try to update Marxism so it can be applied to modern societies and these often have something to say about ethnicity and crime. Other sociologists focus more on racism, which they see as the result of Britain's colonial past. These sociologists see the focus of the police on black criminality as the direct result of this colonialism.

A reasonable account of Marxist ideas is put forward here but the connection to ethnicity is included almost as an afterthought.

Marxism is a structural theory that sees the capitalist economy as the base of society, which determines the 'superstructure' of all the other institutions. How the law and the criminal justice system work therefore depend on the capitalist economy. The working class are dominated and exploited, so they may turn to crime because of frustration or because they want all the things that are shown them by advertising but which they can't have. However, the wealthy are also drawn to crime under capitalism, as it encourages increasing profit and greed. This means that all classes are drawn to crime by capitalism – in the case of the wealthy, through corporate and white-collar crime. Ethnic minorities are no exception to this.

The Item is used and developed and a clear link is made to social class.

Item 2A shows a difference between Asians and Blacks in crime statistics. It seems that both groups are more likely to be stopped by the police and to be in prison than Whites. Marxists might explain this in terms of class rather than ethnicity. They may argue that ethnic minority groups tend to be in lower social class positions so they are likely to be more attracted to crime and more likely to be penalized by the ruling class authorities such as the police, resulting in higher crime levels. Some Marxists would argue it is not ethnicity that results in high crime rates, but their position within the class structure.

Another conflict approach is outlined, more explicitly focused on ethnicity. The explanation given is limited, but there is some attempt at evaluation.

Other conflict theories are put forward by Neo-Marxists who see the criminal justice system and the police as being racist and reflecting a racist society. They argue that higher crime rates for ethnic minorities are socially constructed because the police and the courts stereotype ethnic minorities as more criminal, and so arrest and prosecute them more often. Gilroy says the rates are a myth – ethnic minority crime is not really any greater than white crime, but seems more because of the police and the courts. He says that it is actually a form of resistance against racism, which originated in colonialism. Although this may be true if the crime is rioting and social disorder, this point is harder to see if it is street crime.

Another Neo-Marxist study is the one done by Hall. In 'Policing the Crisis' he describes how there was a period of unrest in industry, and in Northern Ireland by students. As a result, a 'moral panic' was manufactured by ☞

the government and in the media about the growth of 'mugging'. This was seen as a black crime, and Hall argues that media attention was encouraged to distract attention from the problems of the time and to make it easier to crack down on unrest through the law. Scapegoating of the black population prevented people seeing how it was the capitalist system that resulted in high crime rates. Hall argued that it was this capitalist scapegoating that resulted in ethnic differences in crime, so he applied the ideas of Marx about social class to a case of ethnicity. However, this has been criticized, as it takes the side of the criminal and undermines authority. Left Realists say that the differences in crime rates reflect real differences in offending, as ethnic minority groups are more likely to suffer from three factors in crime – relative deprivation and marginalization, and to be members of subcultures as a result.

Conflict theories can be criticized for ignoring the differences in the crime rates between different ethnic groups. For example, some Asian communities such as Indians seem to commit less crime than other groups. They also ignore the many improvements in relations between ethnic groups. Other sociologists, mainly from the labelling perspective, have looked far more at how the criminal justice system works to discriminate against members of ethnic minority groups. For example, they have analysed in more detail the different rates of stop and search, cautions, arrests and sentencing. They have shown much more thoroughly than the conflict theorists how the police focus much more attention on these ethnic groups, especially Blacks.

Overall, this is a reasonable answer to the question, showing some knowledge and understanding of the issues, but it is limited in both breadth and depth. A number of different studies and approaches have been outlined. Some brief points of analysis and evaluation are made and a number of sociological concepts are used correctly. In one or two places a distinction is made between different ethnic groups – this needs to be made more clearly.

Other relevant areas might include: a fuller account of Left Realism; feminist views; artefact explanations (that crime rates are dominated by young, deprived males, and there are more of these proportionately in minority ethnic communities).

It would be useful to explain what exactly is to be included in the category of 'conflict theories' from the start. The question asks about ethnic differences, not about ethnic minorities, so rather more contrast with the white population would be useful. Evaluation could be made fuller by locating the discussion within a debate between perspectives.

Mark: 14/21

A reasonable outline of Hall, with a link to Marx. Some evaluation is provided, though this is rather weak. An opportunity is missed here to use more fully the arguments provided by Left Realism and to show the way in which Hall links to labelling theory.

A reasonable attempt to provide some focused evaluation. Several valid points are listed. The contrast between conflict theories and labelling could be laid out more explicitly.

02 *'Consensus theories such as functionalism provide the most useful analysis of the causes of deviance in society'*
*Assess this view, using material from **Item 2B** and elsewhere.* **[21 marks]**

This is a rather thin account of Durkheim, but a relevant point is made, plus a reference to the Item.

Consensus theories, such as functionalism, argue that there is a common value system that mainstream society follows and deviance is the result of a shift away from these values. However, as Item 2B shows, Durkheim argued that crime and deviance are found in most societies because some individuals have not been socialized properly into the society's shared norms and values.

Merton's strain theory is identified but there is minimal explanation or analysis to show how it might operate. A couple of valid Marxist points of evaluation are included.

Merton is a functionalist and his 'strain theory' explains the motivations behind deviance. He argues that deviance occurs when there is a strain between the accepted goal of society (wealth) and the expected means of achieving this. This theory, created in the 1930s, can still be applied to contemporary trends in crime and Merton's analysis remains influential in sociology today, for example, in Left Realism. However, conflict theorists such as Marxists may argue that the strain theory does not consider the wider power relations in society and it exaggerates working-class deviance. Also, it does not acknowledge the Marxist view that the real cause of crime is the capitalist system.

A criticism of Merton is correctly used to contrast with Cohen and non-utilitarian crime. An opportunity is lost here to explain deviance as a group activity rather than an individual activity.

Merton has been criticized, as he does not explain crimes that seem 'pointless' because they bring no gain in terms of money. Another development of functionalist theory is subcultural theory, which does this. Albert Cohen described 'status frustration'. This refers to the way lower class lads may turn to crime and deviance because they cannot get status any other way. But this is not like Merton's innovation, because these lads turn to pointless crimes like vandalism and joy-riding, as they reject the values of society. This is a subcultural theory because the boys get their status from the subculture – by doing deviant things they get more status.

These are brief descriptions of the three types of subculture; there is no explanation or analysis. It would be useful here to compare and contrast with Cohen and Merton – for example, linking the conflict subculture with Cohen's and the retreatist subculture with Merton's retreatists.

Cloward and Ohlin took this idea further, and divided subcultures into three types – criminal, conflict and retreatist. In the criminal subculture, the members belong to a criminal group with adult criminals. They obey orders and work their way up the criminal ladder. The conflict subculture is where there is no criminal organization, so the young men have their own gangs, usually violent. Retreatist subcultures are double failures, as they have failed in both the criminal and non-criminal world, so they are most likely to turn to drugs.

Several brief critical points are suggested but not developed or explained.

Generally, the functionalist perspective as a whole has been criticized for the assumption that there is a value consensus from which to deviate. Marxist sociologists would dispute this, arguing that it is ruling class ideology, which spreads conformity in order to exploit the working class. Interactionists also provide an alternative argument to consensus theories. They argue that everyone commits primary deviant acts in society, it's just that some don't get labelled. This conflicts with functionalist ideas that the majority of people follow the value consensus. Overall, although consensus theories do provide an analysis into the causes of deviance, it has been disputed by a number of conflicting perspectives.

Overall this answer provides a reasonable outline of functionalist theories and touches upon a number of relevant points. However, the amount of effective explanation is limited. The sections on Durkheim and Merton are particularly thin, but further analysis of all points would improve this answer considerably. Evaluation from other perspectives also needs to be developed more effectively.

Other relevant issues could include: Miller used as a contrast for subcultural theories; failure to explain other types of crime; postmodernist criticisms; recent strain theories; the use of consensus theories as the background for Right Realism.

Mark: 11/21

---

03 *Using material from **Item 2C** and elsewhere, assess the strengths and limitations of structured interviews as a means of investigating the relationship between media use and fear of crime.* [**15 marks**]

Structured interviews have a variety of strengths – they are generally quick to complete and, as Item 2C states, can be used with a wide range of people, allowing for a high level of representativeness. This can provide a more complete understanding of the relationship between media use and fear of crime.

The fact they are face-to-face means the interviewer can write down non-verbal aspects of the interview, such as body language, which could be particularly important when discussing fear. The structure of the questions could also result in high reliability levels, meaning people carrying out a similar study would be likely to achieve similar results. This is because the questions are likely to be pre-coded, which means there is less training needed for interviewers and the findings can be easily quantified. This would make this method appeal to positivist sociologists, as they prefer quantitative material with high levels of reliability and representativeness.

Interviews of any type are more expensive than using questionnaires, but response rates are often better. This is largely because people are less willing to refuse when face-to-face with an interviewer. If people are interviewed in their homes, they are more likely to reveal any fears they have about crime.

Interpretive sociologists would argue that structured interviews are inflexible, as there is no opportunity to develop understanding of the interviewee's views or to follow lines they might want to take. The researcher is imposing his or her own meanings on the questions, which may not ask about the things the interviewee thinks are important. In addition, people may lie about how fearful they are.

However, the issue presented by Schlesinger and Tumber in Item 2C is likely to be a particularly sensitive issue for many respondents, and feminists may argue that the structured interviewing technique is insensitive, and that the interviewer does not give back anything in return. Furthermore, ☞

A couple of strengths of the method are identified and linked to the Item. However, the point is not sufficiently focused on the issue – it could apply to the study of any group or topic.

Several general strengths of the method are raised and linked to theory, but only one is linked to the issue in question – that of the ability to note body language. This point could be developed further.

An opportunity is lost here to focus more closely on the question. Two general points are made, about cost, response rates and flexibility linked to the particular issue only in a loose way. How might the researcher ensure that those interviewed represent all levels of fear? Street interviews would probably leave out many of the most fearful; would interviewers easily gain access to the homes of these people?

The issue of sensitivity could be explored with regard to investigating fear; also the question of embarrassment. Reference is made to the Item. The final point is a general one, which could be applied to any issue.

the presence of the interviewer may mean the respondents alter their behaviour or answers due to social desirability. For example, the admittance of fear may be seen as embarrassing for some. This is known as the interviewer effect and can lower the validity of research. The structured nature of the questions could also lower validity, as it means rapport is unlikely and the interviewer may be unable to prompt or probe into particular examples of fear of crime that may be vital in understanding the issue as a whole.

This answer presents a reasonably good analysis of the strengths and weaknesses of structured interviews. However, there are only one or two places where the writer has tried to link these to the issue of fear, for example, where there is a brief reference to access. The issue of media use has been ignored completely. This is therefore a poor answer.

Mark: 7/15

The answer looks at the method, but not 'in context'. To improve, the focus needs to be on the research characteristics of this issue. Some of the following could be discussed:

- Access to different groups of people.
- Construction of interview schedules – a long list of questions on fear may raise awareness and hence increase fear; it may be distressing to those with high levels of fear; respondents may consequently lie, be embarrassed or exaggerate; these effects may vary according to, for example, gender and age.
- Writing notes or recording interviews may affect those with high levels of fear more, so may not be possible.
- Measuring fear with brief questions may be difficult – how might that be operationalized in simple questions? Unstructured interviews might be more suitable.
- Measuring media use with brief questions – this would need to take into account different types of media and how much of the use is specific to crime. It may be necessary to differentiate between different types of newspapers or television programmes.
- Structured interviews are not likely to uncover the meanings that viewers give to, for example, violence in the media. It would be important to know this to measure any effects. Some may watch crime in horror films but not fear criminal violence; others may have their fear levels heightened merely by watching the news.

All of these points apply a consideration of the strengths and weaknesses of the method to the particular issue in question.

04 *Evaluate different views of the relationship between sociology and social policy.* **[33 marks]**

Sociology, the study of society, is often related to social policy. This refers to the activities of the government to solve social problems and meet social needs. Sociological research has often had an influence on social policy. For example, sociological research on health inequalities and poverty has influenced social policy. Some sociologists such as Peter Townsend have been very keen to see their research determine the way policy goes. He carried out a lot of research on poverty and made suggestions about higher spending on welfare for the poor and the elderly. However, there are a variety of views about this relationship.

> This is a good introduction, defining some terms and containing hints of the possible points of discussion stemming from the question.

Early sociologists such as Comte believed that the purpose of sociology was to study society scientifically and then solve society's problems. From the beginning positivist sociologists thought that sociology should be a science. Like the natural sciences, they would find knowledge about the way society works. With their findings they could provide the government with useful information to help guide their actions. And the hope is that then this would help to make society run smoothly.

> A reasonable outline of positivist views on the subject, linked to the question.

Realists believe that sociologists should be actively involved in making social policy recommendations in the area of crime and deviance. This can help solve social problems, such as political rights and opportunities for education. For example, Left Realists, Lea and Young, put forward results of a local victimization survey and suggested practical solutions to reduce crime rates. However, although Left Realists make policy suggestions, they are often not considered and the suggestions may be limited, due to the influence of government funding agencies.

> One view, Left Realism, is outlined but an opportunity is missed here to discuss other important factors such as government funding.

Liberal feminists argue that anti-discrimination policies often result from sociological research, and are vital in solving the problem of sexism in society. For example, in schools, feminist research on female underachievement led to a number of changes in the curriculum and the way teachers teach. Textbooks are much less sexist than they used to be and there have been projects to increase the number of girls doing science. However, radical feminists don't agree. They criticize this view by arguing that reform is not enough – social problems for women can only be solved by the destruction of the patriarchy of society. They believe that this cannot be achieved by social policy.

> Good use of liberal feminist arguments with a suitable example and some radical feminist evaluation.

It is clear some theorists have a major effect in shaping government policy, for example Giddens' thinking shaped the New Labour government immensely in the 1990s. His idea of the 'Third Way', in between socialism and capitalism, influenced the New Labour government of 1997–2010.

> An area of government policy where some influence can clearly be shown, but this is not developed.

Despite this, many perspectives argue that sociology should not be closely related to social policy – it should be pure, not applied. The New Right believes that the state shouldn't be involved in sorting out social problems, and should encourage individual responsibility instead. This results in less need for sociologists' research. However, New Right ideas have influenced policy a great deal on both sides of the Atlantic, especially in relation to policies on ☞

There is potential for some good evaluation here. Several points are confused, in the final paragraphs: what types of policy might be advocated by different theorists? Should sociologists be advocating policies at all?

tackling crime. Charles Murray argues that families have too many welfare benefits that act to make them too dependent. This produces an underclass, in which lone mothers are not able to discipline their children properly, leading to crime by young boys because they do not have fathers as role models. So they argue that governments should reduce welfare. With regard to crime, they say that the government should have a policy of 'zero tolerance'.

Finally, postmodernists believe sociologists do not have the right to make social policy recommendations, as it is impossible to be completely objective and to identify the whole truth behind social problems. However, they do not provide alternative suggestions on what should shape social policies.

This answer presents a range of different views of the relationship and a broad knowledge of the issue. However, it lacks depth. Coverage of the issues needs to be more detailed. The answer contains some analysis and evaluation, but the possible relationships between sociology and policy need to be unpacked more thoroughly. One major omission is that of Marxist views of the way government policies may help to prop up capitalism.

Government funding is briefly mentioned but other similar factors could be included, for example, government ideology, resources, considerations of popularity, globalization, or the influence of pressure groups.
Mark: 9/15 + 5/9 + 4/9 = 18/33

Total marks: 14 + 11 + 7 + 18 = 50/90 = Grade C

Improving your grade

The following examples show how you can improve your answers to the Methods in Context questions for Crime and Deviance.

---

01 *Assess the strengths and limitations of overt participant observation as a means of investigating police attitudes.*

Weak part-answer

The Hawthorne effect might be in operation. This is when subjects know they are being studied and so behave differently, so the police might not behave the same as usual.

This paragraph looks only at the method. It is not focused on the question and would be true for any study on any group, not just on the police.

Better part-answer

The Hawthorne effect might hamper the investigation, because police officers would be able to prevent the observer seeing the way they treat particular types of offenders on the street, by saying it would be too dangerous for the observer to go out with them.

This paragraph tries to link the limitation of the method to the particular context of the police. The point being made would not apply to any group or issue being studied and refers to some research characteristics of the police.

Good part-answer

The operation of the Hawthorne effect could mean that the researcher is not able to see many aspects of police attitudes. Police officers are well aware of public criticism and may see an outsider as a spy from the Home Office. They could therefore behave 'correctly' when the observer is present or keep the observer away from activities they did not want them to see. As part of their training, the police are taught presentation skills and could therefore make sure they gave the observer a good impression of their attitudes.

This paragraph links the limitation of the Hawthorne effect to research characteristics of the police in two different ways. It is clearly shown how it may present a difficulty *in this particular situation*.

Altruistic suicide	Émile Durkheim's term for suicide in societies where people see their own happiness as unimportant
Anomic suicide	Durkheim's term for suicide in societies where rapid change is occurring
Anomie	Term, first used by Durkheim, to describe a breakdown of social expectations and behaviour; later used differently by Merton to explain reactions to situations in which socially approved goals were impossible for the majority of the population to reach by legitimate means
Anthropocentric	The belief that humans have the right to exploit the environment for their own benefit
Anti-positivist	Rejecting the view that sociology can and should follow the methods and procedures of the natural sciences
Anti-Social Behaviour Order (ASBO)	Restriction on the behaviour of someone because he or she has engaged in behaviour that has proved a problem to others in the community
Authenticity	The extent to which a historical document or other secondary source is real
Bedroom culture	Term used by Angela McRobbie and Jenny Garber to describe the way in which girls are more likely than boys to socialize with their friends in the home, rather than in streets or other public places
Bourgeoisie	Ruling class in capitalist society
British Crime Survey (BCS)	Annual victimization survey carried out by the Home Office
Canteen culture	A term that refers to the occupational culture developed by the police
Capitalism	Term used to describe industrial society based on private ownership of property and businesses
Census	A questionnaire survey carried out by the government every 10th year on the whole population
Chivalry factor	Term used to suggest that the criminal justice system may treat women more leniently than men
Closed questions	Questions that require a specific reply, such as 'yes' or 'no'
Cluster sampling	The researcher selects a series of different places and then chooses a sample at random within the cluster of people within these areas
Collateral damage	Accidental and unintended damage
Comparative method	A method that involves comparing societies to find out key differences that might explain different social phenomena
Compensatory education	Diverting more educational funding to deprived areas
Complementarity	Type of triangulation in which different methods are combined to dovetail different aspects of an investigation (e.g. questionnaires are used to discover overall statistical patterns and participant observation is used to reveal the reasons for those patterns)
Consensus	General agreement

Conspicuous consumption	The idea that identity and status are dependent on material things such as designer labels and jewellery
Control group	In an experiment, the group not exposed to the independent variable
Corporate crime	Crimes committed by companies against employees or the public
Correlation	A statistical relationship between two or more social events
Covert participant observation	When the sociologist does not admit to being a researcher
Credibility	The degree to which a secondary source can be trusted
Criminogenic	Tending to produce crime or criminality
Cultural meanings	The ways in which things are interpreted differently in different societies
Cultural transmission	Values are passed on from one generation to the next
Cyber crime	Illegal acts using the internet
Dark figure	Amount of unknown crime that is never recorded
Deforestation	The decline of forests caused by humans using the land and resources for other purposes
Demonization	Representing a particular group as evil
Dependent variable	A social phenomenon that changes in response to changes in another phenomenon
Desensitizing	Losing sensitivity to, for example, violence in the media
Deviancy amplification	When the action of the rule enforcers or media in response to deviance brings about an increase in the deviance
Deviant career	The various stages that a person passes through on their way to being seen as, and seeing themselves as, deviant
Difference feminism	Type of feminism that accepts that there are key differences in the experiences of different types of women, such as those from different classes, ethnicities and countries
Differential association	The theory that deviant behaviour is learned from, and justified by, family and friends
Domain assumptions	A worldview which is the result of socialization into a particular culture
Domestic labour	Housework
Dysfunctional	In functionalist theory, activities or institutions that do not appear to benefit society
Eco-centric view	The belief that damage to the environment ultimately damages the human race
Ecology	The relationship between the different elements of an environment
Economic reductionism	*See* 'Economic determinism'
Edgework	Originates from Stephen Lyng; refers to activities of young males which provide them with thrills derived from the real possibility of physical or emotional harm (e.g. stealing and then racing cars, and drug abuse)

Egoistic suicide	Durkheim's term for suicide in societies where people regard their individual happiness as very important
Empirical	Based on primary research
Entrepreneurial concern	Way of making money
Environmental crime prevention (ECP)	Right Realist idea that trivial anti-social acts should be clamped down on, otherwise whole areas will deteriorate as a sense of 'anything goes' develops (*see also* 'zero tolerance')
Ethnic cleansing	Forced and often violent removal of particular ethnic groups
Ethnographic research	Form of qualitative research, in which the researcher lives among, and describes activities of, a particular group being studied
Experiment	A highly controlled situation in which researchers try to isolate the influence of each variable – rarely used in sociology
Experimental group	In an experiment, the group that is exposed to the independent variable
Facilitation	Type of triangulation in which one method is used to assist or develop the use of another method (e.g. when in-depth interviews are used to create questionnaire questions)
False class consciousness	In Marxist analysis – the lack of awareness of being exploited
Fatalistic suicide	Results from the over-regulation of the individual (e.g. in a prison or psychiatric institution)
Feminization of the economy	Term used to describe the increase in service sector jobs that are often taken by women
Field experiment	An experiment undertaken in the community or in real life, rather than in a controlled environment
Focal concerns	Term used by Walter Miller to describe key values
Folk devils	Individuals or groups of people associated with moral panics who are seen as troublemakers by the media
Functionalists	People who believe that the main cultural goal should be material success; functionalism is a doctrine that highlights purpose, practicality and utility
Functions	Purposes
Genderquake	Term used by Helen Wilkinson to describe recent radical changes in gender roles
Gender-role socialization	Learning appropriate gender roles
Generalize	Being able to apply accurately the findings of research into one group to other groups
Genocide	Mass killing
Globalization	Process whereby national boundaries become less important
Going native	Researchers becoming too close to research participants and losing objectivity
Green crimes	Illegal acts that damage the environment

Hawthorne effect	Behaviour of research participants being affected as a result of the presence of researchers
Hegemonic	The dominant form of something
Hegemony	The ideas and values of the ruling class that dominate thinking in society
Homophobia	Hatred of gay people
Hyper-masculine	Extreme versions of typical male behaviour
Hypothesis	An initial plausible guess concerning the causal relationship between events
Hypothetico-deductive model	The research process associated with the physical sciences, used by positivists in sociology
Ideological function	Having the purpose of spreading ideas, values and beliefs
Ideological state apparatuses	A term used by the Neo-Marxist writer Louis Althusser for those institutions that he claims exist to control the population through manipulating values (such as the media)
Ideology	Set of ideas and beliefs that justify actions
Illegitimate opportunity structures	Alternative, illegal ways of life, to which certain groups in society have access
Incorporation	Way in which capitalism quickly commercializes aspects of youth cultural style, stripping them of their ideological significance so that they become just another consumer item
Independent variable	In an experiment, the phenomenon that causes the dependent variable to change
Individualism	The pursuit of self-interest
Infrastructure	Term used by Marxists to describe the way a society produces wealth
Institutional racism	Racism that is built into the normal practices of an organization
Interactionism	Shorthand term for **symbolic interactionism**
Interpretivist sociologists	Those whose approach to sociology and research emphasizes understanding society by exploring the way people see society, rather than by following traditional scientific analysis
Interview schedule	List of questions to be asked in an interview
Juvenile delinquency	Crimes committed by young people under 18
Labelling theory	A theory developed from symbolic interactionism, based on the view that deviance is merely a label applied to some people
Left Realism	A criminological theory, which argues that crime is a real problem affecting working communities and is created principally by the inequalities in society, which capitalism causes. Left Realists argue that it is better to work within capitalism to improve people's lives, than to attempt wholesale social change
Liberal feminists	Feminists who see society as patriarchal but suggest that women's opportunities are improving
Longitudinal research	Sociological research method involving studying a group over a long period of time

Macro theory	Way of looking at society, which concentrates on how social structure determines individual behaviour
Manufactured risks	Threats to the ecosystem that are the result of the massive demand for consumer goods and the technology that underpins it
Marginalized	A sociological term referring to those who are pushed to the edge of society in cultural, status or economic terms
Marxist feminists/ feminism	Feminist theorists who base their theory on an adapted version of Marxism; a type of feminism that believes patriarchy is an ideological aspect of capitalism
Master status	When people are looked at by others solely on the basis of one type of act (good or bad) that they have committed, ignoring all other aspects of that person
Materialistic	Focusing on possessions and wealth
Meaning	The word used by Herbert Blumer to describe the sense people make of a particular situation
Media literate	Able to look critically at the products of the media
Meritocratic	System of government or other administration in which people are appointed on merit
Meta-narratives	A postmodernist term used to refer to the structural theories of Marxism and functionalism
Micro theories	Ways of explaining society that focus on how individuals interpret the social world
Moral codes	Sets of rules about what is right and wrong
Moral entrepreneur	Person who tries to create or enforce a rule
Moral panic	Outrage stirred up by the media about a particular group or issue
Moral regulation	The way societies control their members' values and beliefs
Neo-functionalist	Person who favours the updated version of the functionalist perspective
Neo-Marxism	Perspectives that update the ideas of Karl Marx
New Right	Perspective associated with the Conservative governments of Margaret Thatcher, favouring the free market and traditional ways of life
News values	Set of criteria used by the media to determine which events are newsworthy
Night-time economy	Refers to the way a leisure industry has developed at night in certain parts of the inner cities, providing the location of many offences
Non-participant observation	Where the sociologist simply observes the group but does not seek to join in their activities
Non-random sampling	Methods of selecting a sample in which every member of the sample population does not have an equal chance of being in the sample
Non-response	Failure of respondents to return questionnaires or complete interviews
Objectification of women	Treating women as objects
Objectivity	Being unbiased
Open sciences	Sciences concerned with the study of things we cannot see or sense directly

Operationalize	To define something in such a way that it can be measured
Over deterministic	Idea that behaviour is completely controlled by one factor
Paradigm	A framework of thought, which provides the way we approach and understand an issue
Participant observation	Research method in which the sociologist joins in with the group they are studying
Paternalistic	Patronizing approach that removes people's freedom to choose
Patriarchal	Benefitting men; male dominated
Pilot survey	Small preliminary survey aiming to test the methodology before the full survey is undertaken
Polarization	Term used by Marx to describe how, in capitalist society, the rich get richer and the poor get poorer
Positivists	Those advocating an approach that supports the belief that the way to gain knowledge is by following the conventional scientific model
Postmodern	A different perspective on contemporary society, which rejects modernism and its attempts to explain the world through overarching theories. Instead, it suggests that there is no single, shared reality and focuses attention on the significance of the media in helping to construct numerous realities
Prescriptive	Proposing remedies and solutions
Primary data	Data collected by the sociologist themselves
Primary deviance	The act of breaking a rule
Principle of falsification	The testing of an empirical model with the aim of showing it to be false
Proletariat	Exploited class in capitalist society, who sell their labour to the bourgeoisie
Purposive sampling	A sampling technique involving the researcher choosing individuals or cases that fit the nature of the research
Qualitative data	Data concerned with feelings, motives and experiences
Qualitative research	A general term for approaches to research that are less interested in collecting statistical data, and more interested in observing and interpreting the ways in which people behave
Quandary	Problem or source of confusion
Quota sampling	Where a representative sample of the population is chosen, using known characteristics of the population
Radical feminism	A type of feminism that believes that modern societies are patriarchal societies in which women are exploited and oppressed by men in all aspects of social life; radical feminists are feminist theorists (and usually political activists) who see men and male behaviour as the main cause of women's position in society
Random sampling	Where a representative sample of the population is chosen by entirely random methods
Rapport	Trusting relationship between researcher and respondent

Recidivism	Repeat offending
Relative deprivation	How deprived someone feels in relation to others, or compared with their own expectations
Reliable	Refers to the need for research to be strictly comparable (e.g. this is not a great problem with questionnaires and structured/closed question interviews, but can pose a real problem in observational research, because of the very specific nature of the groups under study)
Representative	A sample is representative if it is an accurate cross-section of the whole population being studied, which allows the researcher to generalize the results for the whole population
Research population	The whole group that the researcher is studying
Reserve army of labour	Term used by Marxists to describe certain groups, who are moved in and out of work by the capitalist class as it suits them
Response rate	The proportion of the questionnaires that are returned (could also refer to the number of people who agree to be interviewed)
Right Realism	Perspective on crime that sees crime as an inevitable result of people's selfish, individualistic and greedy nature; associated with Wilson and the idea of **zero tolerance**
Risk consciousness	Term used by Ulrich Beck to describe the anxieties caused by global crimes
Role-playing	Term used by Erving Goffman to describe the way in which people are like actors, each playing a number of parts in social life
Sampling frame	A list used as the source for a random sample
Secondary data	Data already collected by someone else for their own purposes
Secondary deviance	The response to rule-breaking, which usually has greater social consequences than initial rule-breaking
Self	Sense of our own uniqueness and identity
Self-fulfilling prophecy	A prediction that makes itself become true
Self-report studies	Studies in which people are asked to write down the crimes they have committed over a particular period
Service sector	Jobs in retail, distribution and administration
Situational crime prevention (SCP)	An approach to crime that ignores the motivation for offending and instead concentrates on making it more difficult to commit crime
Snowball sampling	A sampling technique which involves finding and interviewing a person who fits the research needs and then asking them to suggest someone else who might be willing to be interviewed
Social action theory	Another name for **symbolic interactionism**; social action theories focus on how society is built up from people interacting with one another
Social construction	In this case, refers to the fact that statistics represent the activities of the people constructing the statistics rather than some objective reality
Social control	The ways in which a society directs the behaviour of its members

Social democratic perspective	View that favours investment in public services and a redistribution of wealth from the rich to the poor
Social desirability effect	Bias in research caused by respondents giving responses they think match the values of the researcher
Social disorganization	Situation where people feel little sense of community or of responsibility for one another
Social fact	A term used by Durkheim to claim that certain objective 'facts' exist in society that are not influenced by individuals (e.g. the existence of marriage, divorce and work)
Social integration	The extent to which people feel they 'belong' to a society or social group
Social interaction	Contacts with other people; people choosing to come together in social groups
Social policy	Has two meanings – can refer to government policy to solve social problems or the academic subject of studying social problems
Social problems	Social behaviours that are damaging to society
Social structure	The way a society is built up
Specialized division of labour	Division of work into a wide variety of tasks
Status frustration	According to Albert Cohen, this occurs when young men feel that they are looked down upon by society
Stereotype	Commonly held but exaggerated and often inaccurate belief
Stigmatized	Labelled in a negative way
Stop and search	Police officers have powers to stop and search those they 'reasonably' think may be about to commit, or have committed, a crime; this power is used more against ethnic minority youth than white youth
Strain	Term used by Robert Merton and other functionalists to describe a lack of balance and adjustment in society
Stratified sampling	When the population under study is divided according to known criteria such as sex and age in order to make the sample more representative
Structuralist theory	Theory based on the idea that society has some 'structure' over and above the interactions of people
Subcultures	Distinctive sets of values that provide an alternative to those of the mainstream culture
Subjective	Personal, based on individual values
Superstructure	Term used by Marxists to describe the parts of society that are responsible for socialization and the spreading of ideology
Surplus value	Marxist term used to describe the profits extracted by capitalists from the labour of the proletariat
Survey	A large-scale piece of quantitative research aiming to make general statements about a particular population
Symbolic interaction	The ways in which people act by interpreting things like other people's language and non-verbal communication

Symbolic interactionism	A theory derived from social psychology, which argues that people exist in a social world based on symbols that people interpret and respond to – labelling theorists tend to substitute the term 'label' for 'symbol'
Symbolization	Associating the dress, hairstyles and music of a youth culture with trouble and violence
Systematic sampling	Where every nth name (for example, every 10th name) on a list is chosen
Techniques of neutralization	Justifications for our deviant actions
Tipping	Process where an area declines once it begins to develop a bad reputation
Transnational corporations	Businesses that operate in more than one country
Triangulation (multistrategy research)	A term often used to describe the use of multiple methods (qualitative and quantitative) in research
Underclass	Term used by Charles Murray to describe a distinctive 'class' of people whose lifestyle involves seeking to take what they can from the state and living a life involving petty crime and sexual gratification
Urbanization	The process of moving to cities associated with industrialization
Validity	Refers to the problem of ensuring that the questions actually measure what the researcher intends them to measure
Value consensus	General agreement on core beliefs
Value free	Not letting personal views influence research
Value judgement	A judgement based on principles and beliefs
Value laden	Inevitably based on personal values
Variable	A social phenomenon that changes in response to another phenomenon
Verstehen	Term first used by Max Weber to suggest that the role of sociology is to understand partly by seeing through the eyes of those who are being studied; similar to 'empathy' in English
Victim (or victimization) survey	Surveys during which people are asked what crimes have happened to them over a particular period
Voluntarists	People who believe that individuals have free will
Welfare dependency	Becoming reliant on state benefits
White-collar crime	Middle-class crime
Zemiology	The study of harm
Zero tolerance	Right Realist approach to crime that argued that the police should aggressively tackle all types of crime and disorder rather than reacting only to serious crime
Zone of transition	Area of city with high level of population turnover